Into the Twenty-First Century

Into the Twenty-First Century

An Agenda for Political Re-alignment

edited by Felix Dodds

GREEN
PRINT

Green Print
Marshall Pickering
1a Beggarwood Lane, Basingstoke, Hants RG23 7LP, UK

Copyright © The Contributors.
First published in 1988 by Green Print
Part of the Marshall Pickering Holdings Group
A subsidiary of the Zondervan Corporation

ISBN: 1 85425 014 0

Text set in Sabon by Watermark, Hampermill Cottage,
Watford WD1 4PL
Printed in Great Britain by Cox & Wyman, Reading

Contents

The Contributors

Felix Dodds, now a maths teacher, joined the Young Liberals in 1974. He was a member of the Liberal Party Council from 1983–6, and chair of the National League of Young Liberals from 1985–7. He is presently active in the Green Voice network of Liberals and Greens.

Mike Harskin is a journalist. He has worked for the Green Alliance, the Campaign for Electoral Reform, the United Nations Association, and more recently in planning. He was vice-chair of the National League of Young Liberals from 1983-6, and Liberal candidate for Brent South in 1987.

Jeremy Seabrook is a former teacher and social worker turned writer and journalist. Born in Northampton, he has been a Labour Party member since the age of 15, but now veers increasingly towards green socialism. His most recent book, *The Race for Riches: the human cost of wealth*, was published by Green Print in 1988.

Michael Meadowcroft joined the Liberal Party in 1958. He served on local authorities in Yorkshire for many years until his election as MP for Leeds West in 1983, a seat which he lost in 1987. He was the party's president-elect when it decided to merge with the SDP.

Simon Hebditch was prominent in the Young Liberals and the Liberal Party in the early 1970s, but left to join Labour in 1977.

He rejoined the Liberals in 1986. He was vice-chair of the Anti-Apartheid Movement from 1978 to 1982.

Peter Tatchell is an author and journalist, member of the Labour Party and the Socialist Environment and Resources Association, and co-ordinator of the UK AIDS Vigil organisation. Since 1983, when he stood for Labour in the Bermondsey by-election, Peter has pioneered much new thinking on the left including most recently a strategy for a 'united, green and socialist Europe'. His latest book, *AIDS: A Guide to Survival*, was published by GMP Publishers in 1987.

Meg Beresford grew up on a farm collectively run by pacifists and first worked as a shepherdess in the Welsh hills. After taking a degree as a mature student at Warwick University, her attempt at a Ph. D. was interrupted by the demands of peace campaigning in Oxford. Since 1980 she has worked for END and CND.

Simon Hughes had been a barrister and a youth worker before being elected Liberal MP for Southwark and Bermondsey at a by-election in 1983. He has been his party's spokesperson on church affairs, on health, and on the environment. From 1986 to 1988 he was president of the Young Liberals.

Liz Crosbie has a degree in economics from the LSE, and now works as a marketing consultant. A committed feminist, she is secretary to the Green Party Council and active in presenting the party to a wider audience.

Hilary Wainwright is a freelance writer and researcher, active in the women's movement since the early seventies, and co-author of the influential *Beyond the Fragments* (1979). She helped create the GLC's Popular Planning Unit in 1982, and wrote a collection of essays on the politics of local economics entitled *A Taste of Power*. She is a contributor to *New Statesman and Society*. Her most recent book, *Labour: A Tale of Two Parties*, was published in 1987. She is a member of the Socialist Society.

Petra Kelly was awarded the Alternative Nobel Prize in 1982 and the Peace Woman of the Year Award in 1983, when she was among twenty-seven Greens elected to the Bundestag in Bonn and one of their three parliamentary speakers. Her book *Fighting for Hope* was published by the Hogarth Press in 1984.

Tim Cooper is a freelance economist, a member of the Green Party and a founder member of the Christian Ecology Group. In 1987 he founded Green Voice, a network of Liberals and Greens, and was a co-chair of the Green Party's Council in 1987–8. He has presented a series for Thames Television, and writes occasionally for The Guardian.

Jean Lambert, a teacher, has been active in the Green Party since 1977, has served on the party's Council as a co-chair, and has helped organise General and European election campaigns at both national and constituency levels. She was a founder member of the Ecology Building Society, and of Play for Life.

Peter Hain was a prominent Young Liberal before joining Labour in 1977, since when he has stood twice for parliament. A leading civil rights and anti-racist activist, he was brought up in South Africa until his teens when the banning of both his parents forced his family to leave. His most recent book, *Political Strikes: the state and trade unionism in Britain*, was published by Penguin in 1986.

Sara Parkin, a nurse by training, became involved in the green movement in the late sixties and joined the (then) Ecology Party in 1978. She has served as the party's international liaison secretary since 1983, and as co-secretary of the European Greens since 1985. She is author of *Green Parties*, Heretic Books, 1988.

Jonathon Porritt became interested in green politics during ten years teaching English and drama in a London comprehensive school. He has stood as a Green Party candidate on seven occasions in local, general and European elections. In 1984 he published *Seeing Green*, and in the same year gave up teaching to take up his present post as Director of Friends of the Earth.

Preface

'We stand today on the edge of a new frontier, the frontier of the twenty-first century; a frontier of unknown opportunities and perils; a frontier of unfulfilled hopes and threats' to paraphrase President Kennedy. At the time that he was giving the speech in 1960, the major concern of the world was nuclear escalation. The twenty-first century brings a host of world-wide problems that affect all of us and how we lead our lives.

The growth of green politics since the 1970's has been enormous, with green MPs having been elected to parliaments across the world. Their agenda, directly related to issues such as the environment, peace, powerlessness and the developing world, is now coming to the forefront of our concerns.

The time scale, and the ostrich-like behaviour of our present political parties and their parliamentary representatives, urgently require the breaking down of traditional Party boundaries. All socialists, liberals, greens, and people who are not members of political parties but who share common values and common concerns for the future of the planet we live on and the way we live our life, now need to come together.

This has started to happen with the recent Green Voice (greens and liberals) and Green Socialist conferences, and the local networking that many liberals, socialists and greens are already doing.

Just as socialism became the dominant philosophy of this century in reaction to the existing political climate, green politics could well become the philosophy of the twenty-first century. Its future is not guaranteed by history, but it is up to all of us to ensure that it has a future.

In March 1988 Prince Charles made a passionate speech calling on political leaders with a sense of vision to save the environment before it is too late. In making this call, he succeeded in summarising the ideas behind this book.

The contributors have taken as their starting places either values, or strategy, or important areas of policy that any future agenda of the left must look at. The book is not intended to be a manifesto for rallying together a new political grouping; we are not yet at that point in history. What it does do is to explore a framework for co-operation, with the common aim of a greener world.

The idea for the book came while I was finishing my term as Chair of the National League of Young Liberals in April, 1987. It fulfils much of the theme of my chairship, that of creating a sustainable green agenda for the left.

I came into politics through the inspiration of Robert Kennedy and Martin Luther King, and the belief in a just and fair world for all of us, where power over the decisions that affect our lives are in our own hands.

Since 1974 I have been a member of the Liberal Party, because I saw that as the best way of achieving my ideals. But no party by itself deserves blind loyalty; if the values which sustain you are no longer shared by a particular party, or are better expressed by another, then there is a need to re-evaluate. For many people the time for re-evaluation has now come.

I would like to take this opportunity of thanking those people who have helped this book become a reality: Carina Trimingham, Kieran Seale, Andy Binns, Andy Reynolds and my wife Rosemary for comments on the contents; Jon Carpenter from Green Print for co-ordinating me; and the contributors, all of whom are very busy people, yet wrote their pieces to a very tight schedule.

Felix Dodds
Asgard, May 1988

Green Values

Jeremy Seabrook

Those of us who grew up within the tradition of the labour movement did our best to sustain that allegiance even when it seemed at its least defensible. Throughout the 1960s, when all the exciting and interesting initiatives were taking place beyond and outside the Labour Party, we still went dutifully to diminished meetings, where the few ageing members re-lived distant triumphs and lamented the fact that so many people failed to use the vote which others had struggled to win for them. In the seventies, while what Mrs Thatcher perhaps presciently described as 'the *last* Labour government' was fighting for survival, we could not avoid the realisation that the party was publicly demonstrating the limits of Labourism. We saw its powerlessness over unbiddable international capital, the beginnings of de-industrialization and mass unemployment in Britain; while the celebrated winter of discontent – which the Conservatives have exploited ever since – was clear evidence to many that the hope of Labour in a society transformed by the heroic struggles of the workers had been terminally disgraced.

It has been the fate of Labour's great myth, relying however distantly on the marxist story of the socially redemptive power of a suffering working class, to become thin and diluted, and to forfeit credibility at the deepest level. Labour has ceased to be the principal vehicle of social hope. Whatever faith may still be placed in the Labour Party, this is no longer the hope of any significant transformation, but the more modest gamble that Labour in power might do better than the present incumbents, at least for the organized working class, that dwindling segment of the population through whom Labour's great ambitions were to have been realised. It is not upon such faint and faded hopes that great political movements are going to be constructed in the light of the realities of the contemporary world.

This is not to deny that the Labour Party contains many committed and passionate people; rather, it is to say that Labour has ceased to be a party of visionary and creative possibilities. It has been drained of its underlying mythic impulse. For a truly energising faith to be effective in the world, there has to be an informing belief that impels people to action. Mrs Thatcher's reputation as a 'conviction politician' is not without foundation. Her faith is in the regenerative powers of capitalism, in the promise of wealth. Her quasi-religious veneration of money is a source of the greatest strength, sustaining and permeating everything the Conservatives do.

Labour, having long ago forfeited any vestigial idea of proposing an alternative social, economic or moral order, is left with the lamest of possible responses – that it will create a fairer, more equal society, with a more just distribution of the same wealth that is created by the capitalist enterprise. This is neither very convincing, nor does it command the passionate support of the people. Labour is handicapped by the contradiction contained in its anti-capitalist rhetoric and posturings on the one hand and the assertion, on the other, that it can make capitalism work more efficiently than its true masters, the Conservatives.

But if the politics of hope have bled away from Labourism, this does not mean that social hope in Britain is therefore extinct. We might imagine this to be the case when we look at the predictable political trajectories of so many of those former radicals who have made the tired journey to the Right, that weary pilgrimage of despair.

It is because the renewal of social hope is a much harder option that so many have sought the easy way out. It is more comfortable to live with a defunct faith than to face the disturbing implications of the new myth that is replacing the doomed belief in transformation through the efforts of dispossessed workers. This new myth is the green myth, the story of the menaced human habitat, the myth that sees in the desecration of the natural base of the planet a reflection of the distortions in the relationships between the rich and poor of the earth. At one level it doesn't matter how much *truth* there is in this view of the world; what matters is that this is how people feel about the way things are, and that this will lead them to action that will radically modify the existing order.

In many ways the green myth may be seen as a reformulation of socialist hope. It too is concerned with the growing inequalities between rich and poor, with sufficiency for all, and with sustainable development. The significant difference is that the green project marks a radical break with the faith in the capacity of industrial society, a faith which the socialists absorbed from the capitalist context within which their objectives were first defined. Although capitalism had many critics in its early stages – horror not only at the disturbance of settled ways of living, but also fear of the violence inflicted even then upon the natural world – the idea that industrialism might finally lay waste the earth was something that could scarcely have occurred to them. The fact that socialism came to depend upon the continuing growth and expansion of the capitalist system means that it can offer nothing more than a judicious hi-jacking of capitalist wealth, applying it to more benign and humane ends than private profit.

If the kind of changes envisaged by the green movement are to be realized, they will require at least as powerful a faith as the malign belief which sustains existing society – that greed is the only effective means of mobilizing human beings. This travesty of human endeavour has become so widespread and deep-rooted that it has become a kind of global religion; so much so that nothing less effective will have the power to dislodge it.

The regeneration of capitalism and the decay of labour are part of the same process. Indeed, the debility of labour is allied to the faltering of the wider socialist project in the world, the growing implausibility of the models of society proposed by Eastern Europe. The growing convergence of the capitalist and socialist economies, whereby each modification of Eastern European rigidities is greeted by the West as evidence that they have seen the light, as an acknowledgement that the capitalist market economies represent the most superior and elegant means of organizing human affairs, is a good thing from the point of view of the greens. While the ideological argument rages around the relative merits of free and state enterprise, this seems to structure effectively all the arguments that matter. The most important question of all is elided – how can existing processes of industrial growth and expansion, to which both systems are irretrievably committed, be accommodated on this fragile and increasingly threatened planet? The eager haste with which the West seeks to encourage every 'progressive' shift in socialist societies only brings closer the day when it will become clear to what extent both apparently incompatible systems underwrite unsustainable predations on the natural base upon which all economic and social systems depend.

While the conquest of nature remained an unquestioned part of the industrial project, it was possible to structure all debate around whether it was or was not inevitable that capitalism would be subverted by those it had called into its service – the working class, those Marx called its 'gravediggers'. This preoccupation was clearly given great urgency by the Russian, and later the Chinese, revolutions in the first half of this century. But the constraints of planetary resources now make this preoccupation seem increasingly sterile; it is rapidly being overtaken by even more urgent considerations and anxieties to do with the survival of humanity itself.

For a long time the environmental havoc wrought by the Soviet Union in its efforts to catch up with the West remained concealed. In 1978 Boris Komarov wrote *The Destruction of Nature in the Soviet Union*, and for the first time it became clear that both capitalism and socialism were united in their desperate assault upon the earth that nourishes us all.

He wrote: 'A Soviet citizen can get a fully detailed, disastrous picture of the state of nature in the United States or the Federal Republic of Germany. He can read in Russian agitated and profound books by Commoner, Grzimek, Parsons or Douglas.

The poisoning of Lake Erie, the oil-drenched beaches of England, and the mountains of garbage in New York even flash before him on the tv screen to convince him of the advantages of his own, socialist way of life ... The Soviet citizen must simply believe the statement that socialism itself, by its very essence, guarantees harmony between man and nature, that "universal ownership of the means of production and of all natural resources foreordains the successful resolution of ecological problems in the USSR".

'In the last decade (1967-77) the incidence of lung cancer has doubled in the USSR. Each year 5 to 6 per cent more children are born with genetic defects than the previous year, and the number of birth traumas and abortions is increasing at the rate of 6 or 7 per cent a year. On the whole, the rate of genetic defects among the population – i.e. the number of people who are genetically handicapped – is today 7 to 8 per cent ... Today's air over "putrid Petrograd" contains about 30 chemically active impurities ... In 1966 a Swedish biologist discovered in Baltic fish and later in the body and feathers of an eagle a very dangerous compound – polychlorinated biphenyls. The world had learned of a new enemy – PCB. The USSR had no knowledge of it; yet concentrations were found at the mouth of the Neman and other rivers, and were later found in every other body of water ...

'At one time famed for its fantastic catches of sturgeon, carp and perch, the Sea of Azov has become a latrine, as it were, for the industrial South of Russia and the Ukraine. The oxygen deficit in the water causes mass asphyxiation and death of fish shoals ... the catch in Azov represents one-ninetieth of what was caught there in the post-war period. It is already comparable with the notorious Lake Erie. Here, at Azov, we have already caught up with America. And gone ahead, since Erie was never the nation's marine larder, as was Azov.

'Around 1975-6, when special soil laboratories were set up, it was found that the country's fields and pasturelands were contaminated with 150 kinds of pesticides, poisonous chemicals and trace elements.

'The mining industry and peat production have ruined no

less than 1.5–1.8m hectares. In Turkmenia unsystematic cattle-grazing on the slopes of Koped-Dag and Kugin-Tag has sharply reduced the growth area of wild pomegranate, pistachio and fig, which play a major role in preventing mountain slopes from becoming wasteland. These plants are just as important in the ecology of local fauna: they provide food for large animals – the wild boar, the wild goat, the gazelle and the wolf – as well as for birds – the rock partridge and the black vulture . . .

'The Rybinsk Sea, once the largest artificial body of water in the world, flooded the best meadows and lands in northern Iaroslav Province, inundating oak groves and other valuable forests. Four hundred and ninety seven villages and seven cities had to be relocated outside the inundated area.

'All the grandiose plans to "harness nature" to divert river courses, to correct "millennial errors by nature" were advantageous for the ruling bureaucracy purely politically, and they became facts. The economic benefits were secondary, and ecology was not taken into account at all. On the contrary, the more such projects contradicted the laws of nature, the more highly they were regarded.

'The example of the Western countries provides no support for the illusion that the problems arising from man's disharmony with nature can be swiftly resolved through religious ideas. Clearly it is only through the development of profound basic ideas about human existence that such harmony, or at lest the alleviation of disharmony, should be sought. But in our society virtually all spiritual literature, all modern philosophical literature, to say nothing of religious literature of various persuasions, is available to almost no one and cannot have any influence on social consciousness.'

When he writes about the assault upon Siberia, Komarov reaches the heart of the issue. It is not just the technological aspects of development, but also the social and psychological aspects which underpin technology, that lie at the heart of our ruin of the planet. Komarov says: 'For a Chuchi or Nenets (the original inhabitants of the tundra), the "dead lifeless tundra" is just as vital a world as France of Greece is for a European, or the Sahara is for a Bedouin. The local deer-herder sees thousands of nuances of life inaccesible to the newcomer. He finds his flocks from their reflection on low-lying clouds dozens of kilometres away; the language of the northern people has not just one word for "snow" – there are dozens of words for snow – blizzard, drift, falling, dry, moist . . .

'Until recently the world of the tundra was for its people a special world, with spirits reincarnated in rocks, in the underground warm tundra, with its myths, embodying truths of human existence no less profound than the mythologies of other peoples.'

One of the bitter ironies of these processes is that at the very moment when the need for sustainable alternatives is becoming apparent, the examples, the living embodiments of harmonious and stable ways of living, are being extinguished. The last vestiges of renewable and balanced traditional practice are being snuffed out by versions of 'development' visited upon them by the triumphant colonizers of the world before they can yield up the precious instruction and wisdom that we need for our own survival. In this ignoble and myopic project, the Soviets and the West are united.

The same story of the destruction of sustainable ways of living comes from the experience of the adivasis or tribal people in India. The adivasis were the original inhabitants of the country, and were designated 'primitive' by the British in order to rationalize their policy of colonial appropriation. They even called them 'criminal tribes' to justify their oppression of the adivasis, who were among the very few to continue the fight against the British until the very end. But a civilization which has survived for millennia can scarcely be either primitive or criminal. It may be wondered whether the adivasis were less civilised than those who cut off the hands of skilled Indian weavers in order to sell inferior British textiles, or than those who destroyed the grain crops of India in order that the poppy might be cultivated so that opium could be forcibly sold to the Chinese.

The adivasis live in equilibrium with their environment. Most do not know how to read or write, but they have a vast

store of knowledge that has been handed down from generation to generation. This enables them to live an almost self-
reliant lifestyle in a tough environment. They have no need to
write down what they know, because the knowledge is commonly owned.

There is a twelve-year-old girl, Raji, who knows the names
of hundreds of herbs, shrubs and trees, and their varied uses.
Many of these supplement her modest diet of cereals and
pulses with essential proteins, vitamins and minerals. She
knows which plants are a source of fibre, which are good for
fuel and lighting, which have medicinal uses. She knows how
to get crabs out of their holes and how to make an ingenious
fish trap. She knows how to catch wild hare, quail and par-
tridges. And because her father is dead, she teaches all this to
her younger brothers and sisters.

Besides being the possessor of a vast system of knowledge,
which includes such Western divisions as animal husbandry,
agriculture, meteorology, herbal medicine, botany, zoology,
house construction, ecology and psychology, she is also part of
a very successful education system in which there are no drop-
outs or failures.

And she is not unique: most girls and boys of her age have
the same, or even more, knowledge. However, there are
increasing numbers who do not have this knowledge. Most of
these attend schools in the formal education system, where
they learn that only knowledge that comes from the West is
valid. The idea that what comes from the school, more distantly from the city, or even more remotely from abroad, is better than what they themselves have is spreading; this is one of
the causes of the loss of self-respect by the adivasis, with their
resultant domination by the rich farmers.

Their agricultural system, often called primitive, is in fact a
sophisticated system that has proved itself by being sustainable
for centuries. Paddy is their most important crop. In order to
provide food security in spite of the unreliability of the monsoon, the adivasis plant more than one variety of paddy, each
with its own peculiar characteristics. If there is a lot of rain at
the beginning of the monsoon they transplant some varieties;

if there isn't, they transplant others. If the monsoon proceeds normally, some varieties produce a good crop; if it doesn't, others do. They also have some varieties that grow on poor land, and others that mature very early. The result of all this is that they always have food to eat within three months of planting the early maturing varieties; whatever the vagaries of the monsoon, they will always have something to eat; if pests attack the crops, not all varieties will be equally affected; and the different times of transplanting and harvesting allow them to make the most efficient use of their own labour.

The adivasis have a special relationship with the forests. Their culture has evolved in harmony with the forest environment, and they are still dependent upon it. They get many vital nutrients from wild fruits and vegetables; many of the medicines used by the bhagats come from the forest. Much of the fuel and all of their timber and reed requirements for housing are found there, as well as the leaves for manuring their fields. Although the adivasis depend on the forests, they by no means degrade them. Fuel wood is taken only in the form of side branches of certain trees; this not only preserves the main trunk, but pruning of the side branches is necessary if the main stem is to grow straight.

Unhappily, the forests which were formerly so abundant and luxuriant have been increasingly felled to feed the timber, construction, paper and rayon industries of the cities. This has impoverished the adivasis, broken the cycle of sustainability, and destroyed the living symbiosis for many of them, a process which occurred so long ago for most of the people on earth. Even their attempts to continue with their traditional living-patterns are represented as despoiling the forests, and they are being criminalized all over again. All this when there has never been a greater need to learn from them.

The truth is that we in the West also live in a dynamic relationship with nature, as do the adivasis or the Nenets. The difference is that our dynamism is one of systematic ruin and destruction. The environment is not something external to us: our abuse of it arises from the way in which our deepest needs have been structured by industrial society. Human need and industrial necessity have become inextricably intertwined, and any disengagement will be a vastly difficult and painful process. This is perhaps why there is something hollow in the anguished exhortation associated with the green movement, and why only the most profound faith will bear us up in the struggle for the kinds of changes that we have to contemplate. The green myth must be amplified and enriched in ways that will make it a living force in our lives, and give us the conviction to bring about the kind of transformation that will be necessary. Rudolf Bahro expresses something of this epic task in his *Socialism and Survival*:

'This is an overall crisis of our civilisation, which is backfiring on human nature. Scarcely has the earlier kind of material want been more or less banished from the metropolises before people are plagued by cancer and crime, heart-attacks and mental illness. The destruction of nature by industrial accumulation, the danger of nuclear war, the impoverishment of marginalized masses in the Third World, mental impoverishment in the metropolises – these are the horsemen of the apocalypse at the end of the second Christian millennium . . .

'Industrialism has already shown that it can no longer offer any perspective of emancipation, simply because it is impossible for all people to achieve. And it has to be halted here in Europe above all, where the industrial system had its start, and where we are particularly susceptible, as also is Japan, to its unforeseen backlash. Unilateral industrial "disarmament" or at least the transition to a quite different kind of equipment is what we need here.'

A Critique Towards Re-alignment

Michael Meadowcroft

Political parties are not cold, static organisations. They are – or should be – movements, whose style and ethos are as influential as their policies. It is therefore crucial to examine the political context for re-alignment. In particular I believe that liberalism has been so badly served by its leaders in recent years that any consideration of re-alignment must concentrate on the nature and potential of modern liberalism and its relevance to a new political agenda. The cause of political change is badly served by those who believe that the present can be manipulated without reference to the past. How the different political forces arrived at their current positions must be understood if they are to be successfully urged to move in different directions. Changing the political agenda from its current Thatcherite domination will not come easily.

The besetting sin of British politics is its superficiality. The public desire for immediate action and its support for simplistic solutions are fed by the media and perpetuated by the political parties. Traumatic events provoke demands for an immediate response, which in most cases ignores a score of other factors and could well be counter-productive. Some politicians try valiantly to deal rationally with such issues, with two paragraphs in *The Guardian*, two lines in *The Mirror* or two sentences on television; others believe that discretion is the better part of valour; and some cynically support openly the populist cries. Week by week, as the decline in community standards continues imperceptibly but cumulatively, so the possibility of peaceful change recedes.

The electoral system we labour under is a massive burden. The greatest indictment of the 'first past the post' system is not that it is undemocratic in that it distorts the wishes of the electorate, but that it is the biggest single obstacle to political debate and thus to evolutionary political change. It enables, even encourages, people to vote negatively against their most disliked candidate and, by discriminating fiercely against third parties, never mind fourth or fifth parties, it forces huge coalitions with a pretence of unity. Such parties have in turn to exercise discipline to enforce a single party line. Thus the attachment of the party 'ticket' to a candidate is a far more influential electoral token than any personal ability or deeply held views.

The economic and social changes of the past nine years have been dearly bought. They have been achieved at the price of social cohesion, and are perched precariously on top of dangerous divisions in society which could at any time threaten the security and stability of our urban communities. Right at the beginning of the Thatcher years Dr George Tolley, then the Principal of Sheffield Polytechnic, spoke of unemployed men and women as 'Those who bear the burden of change for the benefit of society as a whole.' It is not so noble a sacrifice if it turns out that the burden is being borne for one section only of that society. After the 1981 riots Professor David Donnison wrote about *The Fire Next Time*, warning that although it was the inner cosmopolitan areas that currently appeared so volatile, the greater problems were on the huge council estates. If they took to the streets it would be far harder to put the lid on the disturbances.

Under the present government there is an underclass comprising perhaps 20% of the population, far higher in those urban areas which have largely been written off by Thatcherism. High levels of unemployment, declining levels of social security (particularly in relation to help with renewing worn out furniture and essential equipment) and, above all, an increasingly insecure and unstable community, combine to reduce large numbers of decent people to despair. That they have so far not rioted is itself remarkable; the Thatcher 'revolution' has been built on the presumed docility of the dispossessed.

That docility is surprising, particularly given the attempts by the left to manipulate it, but it must not be taken for granted. The Conservatives' arrogance of power, displayed vividly by the social engineering of the March 1988 Budget, is dangerously complacent. For any group of people there is a breaking point, after which it requires only the right demagogue to change a meeting into a mob. That perceptive Quaker Liberal, John Bright, expressed it clearly over a century ago: 'If men build their houses on the slopes of a Vesuvius I may tell them of their folly and insecurity, but I am not in any way provoking, or responsible for, the eruption which sweeps them all away.' Above all it is the feeling of hopelessness, a belief that nothing can change one's lot, that is the greatest threat to democracy. What was applied by President John Kennedy to countries with repressive regimes applies equally within countries where the regime behaves repressively towards minorities: 'Those who make peaceful revolution impossible will make violent revolution inevitable.'

It is significant that the Labour leadership has little idea about how unemployed men and women feel. During the 1987 election there were regular references to 'the unemployed', as if they were a single, impersonal group, as well as constant excoriation of the Conservative Government for putting three million 'on the scrapheap'. That single phrase grates with and angers most unemployed people. No one need be 'on the scrapheap' through being unemployed; it is a curiously narrow view. Employment is very often a key to other life enhancements, but it demonstrates a shameful lack of vision to infer that those without it thereby lack opportunity to contribute to their own life chances, let alone their families' or communities' futures.

I have never believed that it was legitimate to use men and women as wrestling mats in the interests of electoral success. There is a case to be made out for so doing. It is certainly arguable that allowing conditions to get worse for the poor may incite them to revolution and that, conversely, to resolve an individual's housing problem simply enables a rotten housing system to survive a little longer. However, I reject the view that politicians are entitled to manipulate individuals in the interests of some greater purpose.

To do so requires a complete and remarkably arrogant belief that the end result will not only arrive within a reasonable time, but also that it will be an improvement rather than simply different. It also requires an acceptance of the repugnant doctrine that the end justifies the means. Such a doctrine leads to increasing repression and manipulation, because the failure to embed the new order into the hearts and minds of the people undermines the acceptance and stability of the regime. A fearful society is the opposite of a liberal society and, because it is inward looking, it denies the free expression and the 'forum' upon which such a society relies.

There is no alternative to a careful analysis and thorough discussion of policy, however much people – wrongly – feel that they are not capable of such intellectual activity. The failure of all British parties to develop a genuine working class politics is an indictment of our methods and commitment. There is no stable future in a society dominated by middle class males arriving from leafy suburbs to tell the proles how to live. The politics of envy has a strangely attenuated appeal, but the future lies with a philosophy based on equal citizenship in which men and women are respected for what they are rather than what they have or can grasp. The alternative to conservative individualism and socialist collectivism is liberal individuality. Because its prime focus is on the individual and the rejection of economic determinism, only in liberalism can the twin aims of individual freedom and social justice both be achieved.

The resilience and adaptability of families under pressure is remarkable, and whilst it continues there remains the possibility of change without trauma. But the social and economic crisis in many neighbourhoods is so deep as to deny the possibility of easy change. The regular cry from constituents over the years has been for 'less talk and more action', but this appeal is, alas, deeply flawed. The clear effect of political action in our cities over the past forty years is visually unattractive and socially damaging. More involvement by more people, more debate on the potential hazards of the misplaced faith in planning held by both Labour and Conservative governments, could conceivably have saved us from tower blocks, walk-up maisonettes, deck access flats, obtrusive urban motorways, overlarge district general hospitals, and huge comprehensive schools.

None of these was thrust upon an unsuspecting populace with malice aforethought, but each in its way has done lasting damage to a social cohesion that requires human scale institutions. They were part of a received consensus, sometimes referred to as 'Keynesian social democracy', which went with a touching post-war faith in planning. Perhaps this collectivism was a phase that simply had to be endured. Whether it was a result of the consensus or the cause of it is a matter for debate, but significantly it coincided with liberalism's electoral nadir. With Liberals only fighting one-sixth of the parliamentary seats and polling barely 2%, those such as Elliott Dodds and Donald Wade, who resolutely and with remarkable confidence rebuked the spirit of the age, could hardly expect to wield sufficient influence.

As doubts began to stir in the 1960s as to the benefits of high-rise living and the destruction of urban villages, the revival of liberalism accelerated. Jo Grimond was the ideal leader for the time: his intellectual confidence was combined with an attractive irreverence, and presented with considerable charisma. Sadly he was also the ideal leader for the 1970s as well, by which time he was understandably weary of the daily round which was the Liberal leader's lot. By the mid-1970s there was an opening for an alternative politics which the Liberals could and should have grasped. The oil price crisis in 1973 coincided with Fritz Schumacher's *Small is Beautiful*, and with Ivan Illich's insights into social topics.

What was required, and what was eminently possible, was the third renewing of liberalism this century. Liberalism, more than other more prescriptive philosophies, is well suited to adaptation to meet the demands of changing times. In addition to ascribing primacy to human values and the enhancement of the individual, liberalism believes in the 'endless journey'. There is no static utopia for liberals; as one horizon is approached a new vista stretches ahead. Consequently, provided that liberals are well founded in their enduring values, they have much more freedom to explore new challenges and solutions.

Historically it has been liberal thinkers who have first perceived the need to develop new policies and programmes. The Social Liberals such as Leonard Hobhouse and John Hobson, who followed T.H. Green's pioneering work, set out the possibilities for the enabling state as a means of underpinning physical necessities and freeing men and women from many of the constraints which hampered their liberty. The state did not have to be a dictator, but could become a liberator. The disaster of the First World War and the internal Liberal debacles thereafter contributed to the electoral rejection of liberalism, with catastrophc consequences for Britain. By the mid 1920s a further intitiative was required – caustically described by John Campbell as 'The Renewal of Liberalism . . . without Liberals' – which launched the Liberal Summer School as a vehicle for rigorous radical thought. Ramsey Muir, Ernest Simon, Maynard Keynes and William Beveridge participated in an intellectual powerhouse which, among other reports, produced the famous *Yellow Book* of 1928. Once again it was demonstrated that innovation, on this occasion economic, could be harnessed to liberal values. Unlike their successors, the Liberals of the inter-war years lacked no confidence in their basic liberal values and the practicability of applying them to the political agenda.

By the mid 1970s the end of the social democratic consensus was apparent, even if some came to the optimistic belief that it could later be relaunched. The Liberal Party went from 6% in the Gallup Poll in October 1970 to 28% in August 1973. The opportunity was clearly there for the Liberals to grasp. Even if they were unable to hold on to all the latent support at the General Election which followed in February 1974, their poll of almost 20% put them in the driving seat in what was virtually a hung parliament. Sadly, through a combination of a loss of nerve and poor leadership, the Liberals missed the opportunity. Politics, like nature, abhors a vacuum. Margaret Thatcher became Conservative leader in February 1975 and sensed that the country was ready to reject consensus. Thus, from Adam Smith, via the Centre for Policy Studies, Britain got Tory individualism rather than Liberal individuality.

The situation today offers a further opportunity. The key political question is 'What follows Thatcherism?' The past decade has witnessed a transformation of the political agenda. Capital assets have been sold off for revenue purposes and it is unlikely that, particularly with diminishing oil revenues, there will ever be the cash available to buy back the major privatised industries into public ownership, even if it were thought to be beneficial. This denies Labour one of its traditional areas of collectivist action. All parties have to recognise new constraints on future governmental action, and must be intellectually innovative if they are to offer a genuine alternative to the divisive and embittering consequences of Thatcherism.

More than ever, this means that there is no way of achieving any political re-alignment, nor of finding a short cut to defeating the Conservatives, by superficial inter-party arrangements or organisational 'fixes'. The Liberals and Social Democrats went down this debilitating road for seven years, with diminishing electoral returns and with the dire consequences of inhibiting party policy and of stunted strategic development, reflected in steadily increasing frustration and slippage of activity and membership.

At the heart of the parties' problems of identity is the electoral system. The first-past-the-post method exacts such retribution on those outside the two major parties that the pressure to have mass parties is immense. The parties are inevitably too big to have sufficient internal unity and coherence to avoid factionalism. The gap between Sir Ian Gilmour and John Carlisle on the Conservative benches is as wide a chasm as that between Austin Mitchell and Jeremy Corbyn on the Labour side. Each party must pretend to be both uniform and united when, manifestly, they are neither. At any given time one or other 'wing' will be dominant, and it is incumbent on the rest to maintain the pretence of solidarity until they can once again take over the dominant role. The Conservatives fare better under this pressure, because their natural acceptance of discipline keeps more of their squabbles out of the public view.

The public requires three things of its politicians: strong leadership, united parties, and representatives who think for themselves. Even a political Paul Daniels could not deliver all three at once. I believe that the debilitating effect of this on all our political development and institutions is far greater than we realise. Without electoral reform the possibility of an enduring progressive government is remote in the foreseeable future.

Within our present electoral system, merger is the inexorable result of an alliance continued beyond its natural life but terrified of surviving alone. Merger was the aim of the party establishment in both Liberal and Social Democratic Parties, but it was damaged, perhaps fatally, by the decision of David Owen to continue an SDP with sufficient funding and dedicated support to cast a shadow over the purported unity of the merged party, at least until the next general election. Even without the continuing SDP the merged party in its present form lacks that crucial cohesion and political identity that would enable it to mount a formidable challenge at the next election. To go through three different names in ninety nine days is indicative of this lack of cohesion. There are superficial similarities between the two parties, but there are also fundamental differences. It is rather like Rugby League and Rugby Union: both games have their adherents, but one can neither play each code well, nor continue any fixture list, if the teams try to play both at once. For the merged party to succeed it will have to become a Liberal Party, otherwise another political force will fill the Liberal 'space'.

There are those in the upper circles of the Labour Party, sufficiently aware of the temporary opportunity and realising that Labour is unlikely ever to be elected whilst it retains its authoritarian and left wing image, who have been attempting to give the party a Liberal veneer. The 'sensible tendency' within the Labour Party will continue its internal struggle even though there is little or no chance of success. There are a number of crucial differences between Labourism and Liberalism, but the most fundamental is that Labour defines itself by its view of economics; its *raison d'etre* is the collectivism which governs its place on the traditional politico-economic spectrum. Labourism is the opposite of capitalism, whereas Liberalism is the opposite of authoritarianism – of Left *and* Right.

Liberals reject economic determinism as a basis for a political movement, basing themselves instead on a view of people as both individual and communal citizens, for whom the test of the economy is whether or not it enhances their 'life chances'. Consequently, although in terms of *policy* there are a number of similarities, the underlying aims and values are very different. Aspects of the route may correspond, but the destinations are distinct.

The other organic reason why Labour can never assume the genuine Liberal mantle is its constitutional link with the trade unions. In common with most Liberals, I have whenever possible been a member of a trade union. Liberals are instinctively supportive of trade unionism – many of the rights recently eroded by Conservative governments were originally established by Liberal governments – but they reject the myopic binding of unionism with one party as wrong in principle and detrimental both to the party and the union. It is particularly ironic that neither can sever the link, even though a minority of trade unionists has voted Labour at recent elections. The financial and organisational domination of the Labour Party by a handful of trade unions effectively shackles it and erects a considerable obstacle to re-alignment.

Current attempts to move the Labour Party towards 'one member, one vote' are unlikely to succeed if they undermine the union paymasters' influence on the party. In any case, if the constituency party delegates at the annual Labour Party Conference are anything to go by, such moves will simply put more power into authoritarian hands. As Austin Mitchell MP has written: 'More power to party members is not the answer, because the members are the problem.'

There is an understandable lack of awareness of the real nature of the present Labour Party on the part of those who lack experience of the appalling effects of Labour rule of many of our cities and London boroughs. The extent of political corruption employed in the interest of maintaining political control is both thorough and sophisticated. Nor is it a question of the Labour Left alone; the belief in inculcating a one-party state by employment policies, by grant aid strategies and by propaganda on the rates, is widespread. The only apparent difference is that the Left is more open about it.

Because the Liberal Party, alone among the political parties, rejects economic determinism, it cannot comfortably encompass in a single organisation those whose primary motivation is a particular economic structure or imperative. That by no means rules out co-operation both in and out of government in a multitude of ways, but it means that the typical Liberal generosity of spirit is misconceived if it envisages being yoked together in one organisation with those who, quite legitimately, differ on this key point. It follows, therefore, that realignment is doomed unless it recognises two distinct strands of progressive opinion: the libertarian left and the collectivist left. Whether or not there can be any public linkage between them prior to an election is extremely dubious; post-election co-operation has to be an open agenda, with electoral reform being at the top of that agenda and the key to other negotiation.

Historically, Liberal generosity has been unselfish, not to say foolhardy, in its dealings with other parties. In turn Liberals have facilitated the rise of the Labour Party, the birth of the Social Democratic Party, and the need for the Green Party. In 1903 the then Liberal Chief Whip, Herbert Gladstone, concluded a pact with Ramsay Macdonald of the Labour Representation Committee under which candidates would be withdrawn in roughly equal numbers of seats. In the short term it helped the Liberal Party to its massive 1906 victory, but in the long term, by enabling a score or so of Labour MPs to be elected and immediately to form an independent group in Parliament, it unwittingly helped the process under which

Labour replaced Liberal as the main progressive, anti-Conservative party.

The lessons of history were, alas, not learned by later Liberals, particularly by their leader, David Steel. Prior to 1981 his speeches are full of derogatory references to social democracy and its obsolescence, and to the need for all citizens of goodwill to join the Liberal Party. In 1979 Steel aide and speech-writer Richard Holme described social democracy as 'salvation by illusion', and in a book edited by David Steel four years *after* the formation of the Alliance, Ralf Dahrendorf wrote: 'Between the new socialists and the new conservatives, there are the social democrats who believe that by tinkering with the system we can make it work for some time to come. In an intermediate and short-term sense they may well be right, but they have no answer to the underlying issues ... The new pragmatists are merely survival politicians, essentially about the past rather than about the future.' Dahrendorf was right to point out that any possibility of buying social stability and amelioration was snuffed out by the 1973 oil price hike. All pre-1973 strategies were henceforth obsolete.

It was not as if philosophical and strategic warnings had not been sounded *before* the formation of the Alliance. Quite apart from the internal Liberal writers and speakers, a commentator as sympathetic and respected as Robert McKenzie drew the parallel with the 1903 pact and the rise of Labour in an interview with David Steel. One is forced to the conclusion that the Liberal leader had not listened to his own speeches, and did not understand the crucial difference between liberalism and social democracy. Not surprisingly he therefore felt no need to protect and promote liberalism as such.

It is not a question of pride nor of purity, but of effectiveness. The problems of the latter stages of the 1987 election campaign, and the debacle of the merger negotiations, were the inevitable consequence of an attempt to oversell the nature of an inherently unstable and flawed relationship. Of course there were Liberals and Social Democrats who would have been more at home had they swapped parties, particularly in areas where Liberals had previously been ineffective and the SDP had picked up the slack, or in areas where committed Liberals could not face the contradictions of the Alliance and had quietly slipped away, thus weakening the ideological strength of the party. But the roots of the parties were distinct, and the *generality* of their members very different. The result of the errors of judgement of 1980 and '81 are clear: a continuing SDP under David Owen, a merged party low in the polls and, in its present form, lacking the potential of a sharp cutting edge; in short, a long haul back for Liberals.

The separate existence of the Green Party is also an indictment of the Liberal Party, and a result of its lack of confidence in itself. Liberalism has always been based on the quality of life and on the value of the human personality rather than on economic advance. Its great opportunity came in the aftermath of the 1973 oil price crisis, when dependence on economic growth for fulfilment of political programmes was finally and fatally undermined. The party soared in the opinion polls, won a series of parliamentary by-elections, and polled sufficiently well in the February 1974 General Election to deny any party a workable majority. Ralf Dahrendorf's 1974 Reith Lectures on 'The New Liberty' set out a Liberal critique and vision in the light of the new economic realities.

None of this was acted upon by the party leaders, and the October 1974 General Election gave Labour a working majority. Soon afterwards the Liberal Party was plunged into the trauma of the Jeremy Thorpe trial, followed, soon after David Steel's accession to the leadership, by the Lib-Lab Pact. The Liberal *Party* had continued its policy development, particularly on green issues, so much so that the Ecology Party (later renamed the Green Party), which had been formed in 1975, actually debated at its 1979 conference whether or not to disband and join the Liberal Party.

From 1981 the Alliance with the much less green SDP caused considerable heartsearching for a number of Liberals for whom the ecological imperative was a crucial test of political soundness. The merger of the two Alliance parties catalysed 'Green Voice' conferences in January and March 1988 at which members of the Liberal and Green Parties discussed issues of mutual concern. Some Liberals even hinted at possible electoral co-operation, thus continuing the age-old and foolhardy Liberal tradition of generosity to opponents, and falling, for the moment at least, to apply similar tests to Green Party politics as they would automatically apply to other parties: is it an economic determinist party and, even more dangerously, is it determinism centred on a single issue?

If the answer to both is 'yes' then the party is intrinsically illiberal, even if the aim of that determinism is eminently to be desired. The end can never justify the means, and Liberals are aware that an ecological authoritarianism, with zealots attempting to enforce a policy such as population control, could be extremely dangerous and would actually undermine the possibility of achieving important aims. If, as the Green Party asserts, the answer to both questions is 'no', then it is difficult to see how there can be a space on the political spectrum distinct from a genuine Liberal Party. It is the failure of the Liberal Party to assert its liberalism and to have confidence in its own relevance and potential that has caused a number of obvious Liberals to put their political energy and skills into green politics and other single issue campaigns. Jo Grimond was accurate when he wrote that 'a majority of people want liberalism but so far they have not been offered it.'

In the 1940s and 1950s, when liberal values were at their nadir in post-war Britain and planning and collectivism was at its zenith, that a small dedicated band of Liberal leaders, including Donald Wade, Philip Fothergill, Elliott Dodds and Frank Byers wrote and spoke with remarkable confidence that the prevailing political trends were inimical to human values and that liberalism was the answer. It is perhaps the strangest of paradoxes that, as the public began to realise the accuracy of that analysis and once again began to vote Liberal, the Liberals began to lose confidence in themselves. One dispassionate observer wrote: 'Paradoxically, the Liberal Party's eclipse occurred when Liberal ideas gained general currency.' Writing about our present decade, Simon Hughes and Nick Townsend agree, 'It was as though we vacated the pitch when the terms of debate moved in our favour.'

This commentary on recent political history is crucial to the discussion of re-alignment and of what is to follow Thatcherism. The present electoral system encourages negative voting, and the potential effect of such negative voting on a Liberal Party is disastrous. Any suggestion that it is contemplating any pre- or post-election arrangement with either Labour or Conservative wins no extra votes, and immediately sends electors back to Conservative or Labour in droves. Without a proportional electoral system to cushion such swings it is suicidal even to speculate on the topic of arrangements with another party. Unless, miraculously, the Labour Party were to embrace PR – which is unlikely to happen until after its next defeat – one is driven inexorably to conclude that the best hope for the immediate future lies in lifting the character and level of debate across party lines in the hope of changing the agenda by the force of argument.

The agenda for such debate and discussion must be open, and liberals can offer the following subjects for starters:

1. A rejection of economic determinism. Liberal values stem from a view of the individual and his or her relationship with the community; economic structures must serve that primary emphasis rather than the other way round.

2. The vital importance of ensuring that we live in tune with nature and do not exploit the natural world for short-term selfish purposes.

3. Pluralism is crucial to representative democracy, on which the possibility of peaceful change depends.

4. A consensus on procedures – as opposed to values – is essential in a democracy. The end does not justify the means.

5. A rejection of corporatist tendencies, including an exalted view of the state.

6. A diminution and eventual elimination of national sovereignty, an acceptance of transnational bodies and, in the meantime, greater international co-operation.

7. Devolution of power, rather than just decentralisation of administration, so that local communities are able to be responsible for the integrity of their neighbourhoods and to take decisions that enhance stability and security.

8. A fundamental review of trade union structures, roles and affiliations, including discussion of combined committees and plant unionism rather than reliance on the existing hierarchical structures.

It may be starry-eyed idealism to suggest that re-alignment is only likely to be catalysed by rigorous debate with the aim of changing the political agenda, but the paucity of political thinking in Britain affects all of our society. To enter into such debate, party members need to have a deeper interest in political philosophy than is generally the case. To debate across party lines requires both security in one's values and vulnerability about the means of achieving them. For myself I welcome the rare opportunities for such debate. It is high time there was more of it. But, equally, I am convinced that it is liberalism which alone has the answers to a crisis which is more social than economic, and which must be at the heart of any future re-alignment. It is not enough simply to assert it; it must be argued forcefully and persuasively, without arrogance or obscurantism. There are sufficient of Acton's 'sincere friends of freedom' to be an influential and powerful force for progressive policies – if they are challenged directly.

The great Baptist preacher Charles Haddon Spurgeon was once asked to defend the Bible; he refused, saying that all that was needed was to 'let it out'. Its exposition was its defence. I have similar confidence in liberalism's effect in the political sphere. It is high time Liberals gave liberalism a chance.

Liberal Values – Into the 1990's

Simon Hebditch

'Great political leaders are much more than symbols,' wrote the historian A.J.P. Taylor. 'They are individuals, capturing a cause for their own purpose and giving it an unexpected twist.'

The Left in British politics has no option but to recognise the strength and centrality of 'Thatcherism' in the 1980s and 1990s. Any re-assessment of political values and strategies must take account of the intellectual inroads made by Mrs Thatcher's cohorts over the last few years. Such acceptance does not imply that the cause of social justice needs to submit itself entirely to the agenda of the New Right, to the luminaries of the Adam Smith Institute and the Centre for Policy Studies. However, to ignore the social and attitudinal changes brought about by Thatcherism would be to stick one's head into the proverbial sand.

There is a major dilemma for the Left in this scenario. It is perfectly reasonable to re-assert and re-state fundamental values, basing them upon experiences gained over many years of political action and thought, but such assertions should not be seen simply as hankering after cosy, understandable verities of the past. Too often the Left is put in the position of holding on to beliefs and strategies that are perceived to be outmoded. At the same time, history has a great deal to teach us. If Hitler had studied Napoleon's winter military adventure into the vast interior of Russia, he may have avoided exactly the same mistakes and resultant chaos.

It is essential, therefore, to construct an alternative intellectual force that will be capable of challenging the assumptions and aims of Thatcherism. At the moment there is no sign that a vigorous, progressive critique has been developed, and certainly no political programme has yet been enunciated which is likely to galvanise the opposition to Thatcherism. Many had hoped that the energy of this form of conservatism would simply evaporate towards the end of Mrs Thatcher's second term of office. All the usual assumptions were made about her possible retirement from the fray. Once again, this naïve hopefulness betrayed a lack of understanding about her purpose – to transform society so fundamentally that socialism becomes an extinct force – as dead as a dodo. In this context, the Prime Minister hailed Nigel Lawson's 1988 Budget as providing an 'epitaph for socialism'.

What kind of society has Thatcherism created, and in what context should the Left now be operating? Some electoral studies have attempted to show that people's basic values, as illustrated by attitudes to the National Health Service and unemployment, have not been altered significantly over the last ten years. However, this evidence ignores the basic dichotomy exemplified in opinion poll after opinion poll. If people were asked about social issues, they identified the NHS and unemployment as matters of major concern, but such expressions made no difference when the real poll was conducted in June 1987. In other words, concern was expressed about social issues when respondents were interviewed by opinion polls, since this would be regarded as the socially responsible way to respond, but it did not affect the way in which votes were actually cast in the privacy of the polling booth. Put simply, the majority of voters made their political choice because of perceived individual benefits, and because of the endemic fear of the intentions of the opposition.

Britain has become crudely individualistic, a place where enterprise is seen as the desire to climb up the ladder of success at the expense of others, where tax cuts for individuals are seen as preferable to economic measures designed to increase the common good. Ironically, the creation of this more individualistic culture has led to an increase in anti-social behaviour which the Prime Minister, in other contexts, would condemn. We are now a less caring, more selfish, less courteous society. If you create a culture geared to the 'go-getter' approach to life, then you must expect social breakdown to follow. Enough has already been written about the gradual emergence of an 'underclass' of the poorest and most deprived in our community; Britain is heading towards more inequality, not less. But when it comes to the crunch, the majority of people in work are relatively better off than they were five years ago and see no reason to risk this position.

Liberal values and beliefs challenge the crude aspects of individualism, and the patronising, sometimes directive, contents of state socialism. Liberalism is grounded in the rights and responsibilities of the individual. Individual freedom is a prerequisite of any liberal society, and a liberal society is a prerequisite for social progress for all sectors of society. Radical liberalism grew out of the struggles of the eighteenth and nineteenth centuries to extend the boundaries of freedom. The collapse of authoritarian monarchical government, the demise of the overweening influence of the aristocratic houses, and the consequent moves towards political organisation amongst ordinary people became the seedbed of both socialist and radical liberal developments. The growth in political activity between 1790 and 1830, firstly through the influence of the French Revolution and the Napoleonic Wars and subsequently in relation to the development of industrialism, had a major bearing on the activities of the popular movements in the nineteenth and twentieth centuries.

Liberal values have long been associated with individual freedom. Freedom is the bedrock of liberalism, the very essence of the accumulated nostrums and perceptions of Liberals over the years. The emergence of the Social and Liberal Democrats in March 1988, and the consequent official death of the Liberal Party, in no way diminishes the strength and purpose of Liberal beliefs. A political party is only a mechanism for promoting and putting into effect the commonly accepted views of groups of individuals. Whether the SLD will be able to nurture and extend the growth of liberalism will be tested in the next two years, but if it is to succeed, all those with genuinely radical

liberal ideals will have to play their part in attempting to ensure
that the SLD becomes a force for radical change rather than a
rest home for played-out social democrats.

Liberals have always accepted that there is both negative
and positive freedom – freedom from want, hunger and
oppression, as well as the freedom to participate in the organisation and development of society. It is the setting of freedom
as the first element of a political philosophy that distinguishes
liberal values from those espoused by the New Right and state
socialism. As Alan Beith, Social and Liberal Democrat MP for
Berwick, has said, 'A Liberal society sets freedom first. Marxism does not, and Thatcherism does not.'

Liberal values start from the importance of individual
human beings, the spiritual uniqueness of human personality,
and the right for all to be involved in the process of determining
the future direction of their communities. Marxism holds to an
economically determinist mode of thought which sees individuals only in relation to their economic position and, therefore, lays itself open to the Leninist and Stalinist distortions
that we have witnessed over the last eighty years. Thatcherism
is also a philosophy predicated on a strictly economistic view
of life, which is why the rhetoric of the enterprise culture can
apparently stand side by side with the realities of life for the
country's poorest – the growth of the disparities of wealth and
the assumption that to extend 'choice' is to enhance freedom
and the sum of human happiness. In recent years we have been
regaled by the concept of 'consumerism' and, within this context, the extension of choice. Once again, the selection of the
term 'consumerism' illustrates the economic way in which life
is being viewed: participation implies the ability to buy the
good things that are available, the helter-skelter rush for more
and more credit, and the belief that an individual's value is
determined solely by access to Volvos and videos.

Thatcherism has recently made the 'extension of choice' one
of its principal Parliamentary maxims, extending the notion to
education, housing, and local government reform. But choice
is only any use if it is effective and informed, and as long as it
can be afforded. The sort of choice offered by Thatcherism is

no choice at all, as Paddy Ashdown, Social and Liberal Democrat MP for Yeovil, wrote recently: 'But the so-called choices of Thatcherism are choices for the few, not for all; for the privileged, not for the dispossessed; for those whom wealth has made free, not for those trapped in poverty, disability or misfortune. If this is the age of individualism it is also an age when, once again, individual liberty is the key value. And, if choice is the new form of liberty, our task is to provide it not just as a privilege for the few, but as a right for all.'

The liberal values of freedom and individualism do not imply selfishness. These values are complemented by others relating to a communitarian approach to life – one's own freedom is limited by one's responsibility to others and to the common good. Liberals have pioneered community action and community politics as being intrinsic elements of a liberal philosophy. But marxist-leninists claim the same. In terms of beliefs, they would argue that they are intent on the development of human personality and individual fulfilment, but that these states of 'nirvana' can only be achieved through collective action and collective responsibility. Marxism failed not only because of its inaccurate economic predictions, but also because it led to the elevation of the revolutionary party above the interests of the people. The revolutionary party came to believe that it automatically represented the best interests of the working class and need not, therefore, actually involve the masses in political struggle.

The essence of the strategic dispute between the Bolsheviks and the Mensheviks in Russia between 1902 and 1917 was precisely the extent to which it was possible to transform an oppressed, feudal society either through the operation of a tight, secretive organisation (as represented by the Bolsheviks) or through mass participation in the struggles of daily life (as favoured by the Mensheviks). The trouble with the former approach is that while it is clearly an attractive option in a revolutionary situation, it is then virtually impossible to sweep away the secrecy and dictatorial methods at a later stage. The way open for directed labour, the elimination of class enemies, and the creation of a stalinist mode of government – a way the

Soviet Union and Eastern Europe followed between 1917 and 1986.

Radical liberalism has attempted to find its way through this ideological minefield. The development of theories of community politics since 1970 has been part of this process. There are three elements necessary in a liberal political philosophy: the primacy of individual freedom; the centrality of the individual's responsibility to both the immediate and the wider community; and the experience of genuine participation in decision-making. Only liberal values have something to say on all of these elements.

Community politics is participation in collective action within specific communities, in order to transform both material and spiritual aspects of life. It is the affirmation of the importance of ordinary people, and their ability to influence local policy and resources. Put at its most powerful, the concept has been defined as encouraging people to 'take and use power for themselves'.

Some of the ideas about popular control and community sovereignty emerged from the socialist tradition. The Institute for Workers' Control, an organisation once regarded with great suspicion by the Labour Party, formulated the concept of workers' control, since amended to 'community control'. Writing in 1970, Victor Anderson said: 'All this has been summed up in the slogan "community control", which I think is a good one – control of workplaces by the workers there, not by boards of directors; control of schools and universities by the staff and students there, not by boards of governors; control of neighbourhoods and housing estates by people who live there, not by remote councillors and council officials.'

A concomitant of the community politics approach is the development of policies of devolution and decentralisation of power. The essential liberal element is the decentralisation of power – not the decentralisation of service delivery which we have seen in many local areas. Given that liberals are concerned to spread power and influence, we are bound to favour moves to take power away from the centre and vest it in local areas and economic units.

Liberal values will lead to a radical extension of devolved decision-making by highlighting the role of regional government in England, creating a Scottish Parliament and a Welsh Assembly, moving appropriate departments of state out of London, and enabling local authorities to wield greater influence over their destinies. Thatcherism, whilst mouthing the rhetoric of freedom and local autonomy, has consistently chipped away at local discretion, reducing the ability of local authorities to plan strategically for social and economic development. Some Labour local authorities have interpreted community politics as meaning the promotion of their own political perspectives. The interests of local people are often lost in this 'right on' approach. You cannot generate a real and lasting transformation of society without galvanising the free adherence of the majority of people to the proposed changes. Anything less simply replaces one unrepresentative clique with another.

Unfortunately it cannot be assumed that liberal community politics has always been free of self-interest and distortion. It can easily fall into the trap of being an electoral mechanism designed to enlist the interest and allegiance of the voters, rather than a set of values defining the whole of our politics, both personal and institutional. There have been many examples of such manipulation, as well as illustrations of good practice.

Taken as a whole, the liberal values of community, participation, methods of government, community and worker control, and the effective decentralisation of power, combine to produce the most radical set of political proposals on offer within current British politics. In the industrial and employment sphere, liberal values assert the right of workers to participate in decision-making regardless of the ownership situation. Profit sharing and a financial stake in a company's future are undoubtedly beneficial both to the company and its employees, but the primacy of the right to participate is a prerequisite of industrial democracy. Opening up company books to employees, the formation of genuine workers' councils which can decide on the future direction of the company, including its investment, wages, sales and marketing policies, are the direct result of liberal values which emphasise the central importance of both individual freedom and collective involvement. This fundamental premise provides a meeting point between liberal values and liberalised and libertarian versions of socialism, as exemplified by recent developments in Eastern Europe, the Soviet Union and China.

The marxist-leninist movements have discovered that capitalism has not collapsed, and that it continues to hold economic and political sway throughout vast sections of the industrialised world. In fact, the march of political history towards socialist transformation has been halted in its tracks. Economically, state socialism has widely been found to be disastrous. The 'glasnost' and 'perestroika' reforms in the Soviet Union are being led by economic necessity; China has rejected the maoist road and confirmed that what the country needs is a good dose of capitalist development; and a number of Third World Countries, including Mozambique and Tanzania, have been hampered in their development by hidebound approaches to state socialist methods of political and economic organisation.

Over the last thirty years there have been three major movements for socialist renewal and reform within Eastern Europe. Each, while failing in its immediate objectives, has provided real lessons for the task of finding a synthesis between libertarian socialist values and liberal values. That such a synthesis exists is beyond dispute, but it must be argued and developed in a coherent manner. Some of the theoretical underpinning of marxism acknowledges the importance of liberty and freedom, but the experience of leninist approaches in the twentieth century has emphasised the economic basis of society and the elements of class exploitation endemic in crude capitalism.

One of the central themes of the revolution in Hungary in 1955–56, the Czechoslovak 'Prague Spring' of 1968, and the Polish Solidarity movement of 1979–81, was the absolute necessity to re-assert the fundamental human values of these societies. The Czechoslovak renewal was described as 'socialism with a human face', thereby implying that one practical effect of normal socialist practice was to be dehumanising. 'The Czechoslovak debate on this subject was markedly different, wrote Jiří Pelikan in 1971, in that it laid the main emphasis on the creation of actual guarantees to enable democracy to work in practice. Czechoslovakia was concerned with the practical safeguarding of the autonomous position of the various components of the political system and with the creation of conditions under which public opinion could really make itself felt, so that the ruling elite could no longer interfere with the fundamental civic rights of the individual.'

In all three cases, the impetus for reform was provided by the need for economic change and the consequent desire for greater liberalisation and democracy. The Soviet invasion of Hungary in 1956 put paid to the first example. The repeat performance in Czechoslovakia in 1968 ended a vital period of internal socialist renovation not dissimilar to Gorbachov's current efforts in the USSR. The Polish Solidarity movement, whilst also imbued with other cultures and forces, also had a major impact, to be silenced by Jaruzelski's imposition of martial law – a step seen as preferable to being on the receiving end of yet another Soviet military adventure.

In terms of liberal and libertarian socialist values there was a further aspect of these three events which was of major importance – the similar approaches taken to building the opportunities for direct democracy and workers' control at workplace level. Study of the 1956 events in Hungary highlight the demands of people for more control over their everyday lives, especially in relation to the way in which their factories were operated. Workers' Councils were set up throughout Budapest and in all major cities and towns, and such bodies not only advanced the cause of workers' control, but also provided a forum at which wider political and social issues were debated. Exactly the same phenomenon occurred in Czechoslovakia in 1968 and in Poland in 1980–81. The huge growth in Solidarity was based on large factories in cities like Warsaw and Gdansk, and later spread to the more agricultural areas. The workplace became the focus of reform, renewal and, when necessary, challenge to the political authorities.

The common themes of direct democracy and workers' control, linked to the active debate on the future of their respective countries, must not be ignored by those attempting to find a synthesis between aspects of socialist ideology and the primacy of liberal values. We know that we are on the right track when stalinists and neo-conservatives start worrying about the degenerate influence of 'bourgeois liberalism', as happened during the Chinese 'Democracy Wall' demonstrations of 1985–6!

The last important aspect of liberal values is the need to promote and defend pluralism. Returning to the domestic scene, it is pluralism which has been most at risk from the authorities of both the New Right and the Hard Left. While pretending to favour a libertarian approach, the gurus of the New Right are actually trying to construct a society which is restrictive and monolithic. The fact that Mrs Thatcher wants to 'eliminate socialism' is a sign of massive intolerance.

Political ideas and directions must be tested against each other; a political market place should exist where people with very different views can present their cases for public consumption, rather than assuming that one set of ideas is anathema and cannot be contemplated. This intolerance seems to be shared by both political extremes. In the years since 1981 the perspectives and programmes linked to the Bennite Left of the Labour Party have gradually been warped and transformed by the way in which politics have been practised, but hatred and intolerance have no place inside a political movement. Undoubtedly there is also a section of the Labour Party which takes a leninist position – that a 'tightly-knit group of politically motivated people' have the right to speak on behalf of the population and take action on its behalf. Such simplistic views have led to sections of the Labour Party believing that all they had to do was to occupy the positions of power within the party and trade union movement, cause industrial and social chaos, and thereby bring about a 'revolutionary' situation. Whether such tactics ever had sufficient public support was regarded as unimportant by those who believed in the insurrectionary road to political power.

The pressures created by the 1984 miners' strike illustrated this issue. It was clear that the miners were not a united force, but no steps were taken to ballot the national membership as a whole. The legitimacy of the strike was always in question, and some believe that the tactics used were politically suspect. Jimmy Reid, one of the leaders of the Upper Clyde Shipbuilders work-in in 1971, said: 'The danger to the Labour movement stems from "Scargillism", which, if it is anything, is the politics of seizing power, not winning it through the democratic process.'

Rigidity, intolerance, and a bureaucratic disregard for the real concerns of people are the enemies of liberal values. The absolute political imperative at the current time is to create a campaigning coalition of interests opposed to the fundamental dangers posed by Thatcherism. Taking account of all the problems, and of the inbuilt diversity of concerns represented by the different political parties, it is necessary to build a force that stands a chance of unseating the Conservative Government in 1991–92. This means once again resurrecting the desire for a realignment of the Left, but it must be a realignment of the 'democratic' Left, prepared to work together in a common cause.

Political re-alignment is often assumed to consist solely of the creation of some sort of united force across the traditional spectrum of socialist and liberal movements. A whole new dimension has entered British politics recently which needs to be taken into account – the emergence of green politics. The green perspective, incorporating an environmental and ecological approach within a political programme, together with the associated arguments pertaining to the creation of a stable state and a sustainable economic structure, will play a major role in the forging of a political realignment of the democratic left.

As with many political developments, this country seems to be lagging behind the social movements of other industrialised countries. The Greens in West Germany have been a significant force for some years, and the 1988 French Presidential elections witnessed the growth of progressive politics as well as the more unseemly elements represented by the French National Front.

Any such realignment in Britain has to be built on liberal principles and values, and has to unite around common themes – the enhancement of local democracy in all its forms, the creation of a crusade against poverty, the generation of effective participation both in local communities and places of work, and the extension of real freedom and choice to all, not just the privileged. This is a radical agenda, and it is based upon fundamental liberal values. As Bernard Greaves has written, such values can help to change society: 'The key to transforming society must, therefore, rest in a movement which promotes diversity, experimentation and spontaneity. The movement itself is the embryo of the new society, and those who take part in it must start the process of transforming society by transforming their own awareness, life-style and relationships . . . centralised and authoritarian power structures must give way to people sharing in democratic decision making at a local level.'

Ecological Sustainability

Peter Tatchell

The green movement is, without a shadow of doubt, the most important new radical movement since the emergence of socialism nearly two centuries ago.

It alone has fully understood the potentially exterministic effects of the escalating ecological crisis, and it alone has developed a coherent and radical critique of accepted capitalist wisdom prior to the advent of the green movement.

Armed with a new theoretical and conceptual framework, the green movement has identified the existence of an emerging ecological disaster involving the rapid depletion of the Earth's finite natural resources and the gradual poisoning of the air we breathe, the water we drink, and the food we eat.

Even more importantly, it has proffered unique and ultimately revolutionary solutions to these problems which involve the fundamental reorganisaton of society around the principle of ecological sustainability – the care and conservation of the natural environment and its resources to ensure the biological and social reproducibility of the human species.

Despite its relatively short period of existence, the green movement has already created an unprecedented public awareness of ecological issues, and has influenced the orthodox political agenda accordingly. All the mainstream parties – both on the left and on the right – have been forced to acknowledge, however superficially, that ecology is now a significant political issue.

As the scale of ecological devastation intensifies and its possibly cataclysmic long term consequences become more clear, the ecological crisis is likely to emerge as one of the most central and controversial issues of future political debate. Furthermore, faced with the prospect of apocalytic resource scarcity and environmental degradation – including potentially irreversible climatic and genetic changes to the infrastructure of the biosphere – this crisis will almost certainly provoke dramatic political redefinitions and realignments in terms of what is considered progressive and what is condemned as reactionary. It may well, over time, result in the coalescence of a new radical green political bloc which transcends party boundaries, and which embraces ecologically-enlightened people from all the existing political groupings.

The very real threat to human survival which is unfolding around us is not only likely to provoke new-found common ground and greater co-operation between radical greens, liberals and socialists; it may eventually convince many hitherto conservatively-inclined people that radical political measures are essential to ensure the long term sustainability of our society and our species.

The creeping ecological catastrophe, which has steadily become more and more apparent over the last two centuries in parallel with the advance of capitalist industrialisation, involves two key dimensions which jeopardise the continued existence of human life on this planet: the ruinous decimation of the natural environment, and the rapacious exploitation of the Earth's limited and irreplaceable natural resources.

The sheer scale of existing and imminent environmental degradation is nightmarish in the extreme. The rapid destruction of tropical rainforests – the 'lungs' of our planet which convert poisonous carbon dioxide into life-giving oxygen – may eventually change the balance of elements in the Earth's atmosphere, and thereby limit our planet's oxygen-producing and species-sustaining capacities. As we have already seen in Brazil, the mass felling of rainforests is also causing severe local and global climatic changes, massive soil erosion and denutrification which is making farming in the forest-cleared areas almost impossible, and causing widespread hunger, forcing millions of people from formerly self-sufficient agrarian communities to migrate to overcrowded urban slums.

Acid rain, which is largely and knowingly caused by sulphur dioxide emissions from fossil-fuelled power stations, is estimated to cause £3,000 million damage a year in Europe alone. It is slowly killing forests and lakes and the wildlife within them. It is also harming crops and livestock and resulting in a decline in food production in the worst affected areas.

With the depletion of the protective ozone layer – primarily as a consequence of the use of chlorfluorocarbons – the increased penetration of ultra-violet light is likely to cause a huge rise in human cancers and allergies, leading to many deaths and much suffering, requiring the outlay of vast additional expenditure on the public health services. The growing levels of ultra-violent light may eventually also precipitate a long term decline in world fisheries, livestock and agricultural production, thereby adversely affecting global food supplies and contributing to increased famine and starvation.

Through the 'greenhouse effect', whereby the thick band of pollution in the upper atmosphere prevents the escape of Earth-generated heat into outer space, average global temperatures will probably begin to rise in the early twenty-first century. This could turn many existing arable lands into barren deserts incapable of supporting agriculture and, for that matter, human life. It could partially melt the polar ice-caps, causing the flooding of dozens of fertile low-lying countries and the displacement of hundreds of millions of people onto other, less productive, parts of a shrinking and already overcrowded global land mass.

Perhaps most alarming of all, the essential genetic basis of the human species is now threatened by the constant and cumulative effects of low-level radiation releases from nuclear energy plants, high-voltage power lines and nuclear weapons tests. The long-term effects of this exposure to radiation is summed up by Dr Rosalie Bertell in her book, *No Immediate Danger*: 'The wear and tear caused by radiation results in the gradual accumulation of mistakes in the body's homeostatic mechanisms; for example, we may no longer be able to produce an antibody to counteract some environmental irritant, so we become 'allergic'; or, our cells multiply without having the sense enough to rest, and we get a tumour . . . It can also injure the ovum and sperm cells from which all future generations derive . . . With milder damage – such as asthma, allergies, juvenile diabetes, congenital heart defects and sense organ and motor dysfunctions – the individual can live a semi-normal life and perpetuate the damage in succeeding generations . . . Radiation can both increase the proportion of slightly damaged people in the population and also make their survival more difficult.'

Similar minor genetic disorders and mutations are also being caused by the contaminaton of drinking water with carcinogenic nitrates and aluminium sulphate; neurotoxic lead emissions from car exhausts and lead water piping; the adulteration of manufactured food with harmful colourings and preservatives; and the accumulation in the food-chain of residual herbicides, antibiotics, hormones and pesticides used in agriculture and livestock farming.

Dr Bertell's conclusion about the long-term effect of radiation exposure is equally applicable to these other environmental toxins. Over generations, she suggests, exposure leads to incremental genetic damage and the progressive debilitation of the human species: 'The defective offspring will in turn produce defective sperm or ova, and the genetic "mistake" will be passed on to all succeeding generations, reducing their quality of life until the family line terminates . . . through eventual infertility and/or death prior to reproductive age. On a large scale, such a process leads to selective genocide of families or species suicide.'

This, then, is the ultimate apocalyptic threat that environmental degradation, in all its various forms, poses to the future sustainability of human civilisation.

It is not, however, the only apocalyptic threat which the ecological crisis embodies. The second, and equally fearful, dimension of that crisis concerns the rapid exhaustion of our planet's stocks of finite natural resources, which comprise the building blocks of our technological and social organisation.

In the last two hundred years alone – a mere fraction of

human existence – capitalist industrialisation by a handful of countries in Western Europe and North America has resulted in a massive depletion of the Earth's non-renewable minerals and other natural resources which took millions of years to form and accumulate.

Already, the enormous expansion of production and consumption since the late eighteenth century has led to a situation where the supply of many vital raw materials such as tin, aluminium, copper, lead, zinc, tungsten and mercury may begin to run out in fifty to a hundred years' time. Even such critical resources such as coal and oil, which currently exist in relative abundance and are the energy power-horses of our economies, will be in short supply a little more than a century from now.

The precise dates of resource diminution are, of course, difficult to pinpoint because of various imponderables, including the possibility that Third World economic development may hasten resource scarcity and the possibility that the discovery of new reserves of raw materials may delay it.

What is certain, however, is that the crisis of resources is sooner or later bound to become a major global problem which threatens the sustainability of our economy and the whole cultural superstructure which has arisen from and is supported by it.

All the signs are that consumer demand will proliferate unabated in the West, and that more and more Third World countries will begin the process of industrialisation in pursuit of a higher living standard for their peoples.

Given the vast devouring of global raw materials which has already occurred in the course of industrialisation in the European-populated pockets of our planet, it seems inevitable that a major upsurge in economic development in the poorer nations – which is entirely justified and necessary given the immense scale of human suffering which flows from their present impoverishment – is certain to accelerate the crisis of resources.

Imagine the grotesque consequences – not only for resource availability, but also for environmental preservation – if all the world's nations industrialised to the same degree as the West, using the same massive volume of resources. Think what would happen if the two-thirds of the Earth's population who live in the poorer countries demanded their right to food, water, electricity, schools, hospitals, public transport, houses and consumer durables on an equal basis with people living in the industrial countries. Is that not their right?

Yet such an explosion of demand would place an intolerable strain on our planet's finite resource base. It would simply not be able to cope.

Irrespective of this scenario, and regardless of when or if Third World countries begin industrial take-off, there will come a time when even the existing levels of economic activity in the West – without any further economic growth – will be sufficient to generate the devastating depletion of many basic raw materials.

When supplies of these materials begin to run out, become excessively costly to extract, or simply cannot be produced in adequate quantities to meet rising global demand, our economies and whole way of life will face potential collapse.

The prospect of being unable to sustain an accustomed level of economic output, consumer spending and material prosperity is certain to intensify the competition for control of diminishing resources. Desperate to retain their privileged positions in the world economy, the rich industrial nations and their powerful manufacturing corporations will become locked in a fierce struggle for control of fewer and fewer raw materials. This struggle is likely to be a two-way battle, both against other industrial states and their multinational offshoots, and also against attempts by the poorer countries to seek a fairer cut of global resources.

In these circumstances, there is a very real possibility that the world will be torn apart by a series of ruthless and genocidal inter-imperialist wars, in which whole populations and nations become expendable in the mad scramble for scarce natural resources.

Herein lies the second truly apocalyptic danger posed by the emerging ecological crisis – the rapid dissipation of the Earth's restricted reserves of non-renewable raw materials which, together with the wholesale degradation of the environment, is unsustainable and threatens to plunge our societies into an economic and military barbarism.

As more and more people become aware of this ecological crisis and its truly fateful possibilities, there is bound to be a burgeoning of green consciousness and a profound rupture of orthodox political alignments. The urgency of preventing an ecological Armageddon could precipitate a coming together of green-spirited radicals from all the progressive political traditions, based around a common commitment to an ecologically sustainable future.

The present trend towards ecological exterminism is a generalised and pervasive assault upon all of humanity, and upon the entire natural world of which we are all a part and on which we all depend for life. It threatens everyone regardless of class, region, gender, religion, nation, race or sexual orientation.

This is the universal message of the green movement: we are *all* harmed by the ecological crisis and therefore we *all* have a common interest in uniting together with people of *all* classes and *all* political allegiances to counter this mutually shared threat.

The basis of this unity must involve the rejection of class and national privilege. Vested economic interests cannot be allowed to stand in the way of a solution to the crisis of resources and pollution. Fairness dictates that for the sake of the common good those with the greatest wealth will have to make the greatest sacrifices; and those who presently monopolise the economic power and authority which is impelling our society towards ecological catastrophe will have to surrender that power and authority to democratic decision-making and public accountability.

The bottom line is that biological existence is the precondition for the existence of society, and that economic sustainability is the precondition for the sustainability of culture. Without the natural environment and resources to support human civilisation, there can be no capitalism and no socialism.

Indeed, there is no point even beginning to contemplate any humanitarian goal or social utopia unless we have a planet capable of sustaining human life.

This recognition, for so long evaded or denied by the pre-green movement parties of the right and the left, is the potential driving force for a thorough-going social revolution, and the basis for the radical political realignments which are necessary to make that revolution possible: the creation of a new green consciousness, the construction of a new green policy agenda, and the forging of new green alliances which cross class and party boundaries to unite the overwhelming majority of the people behind a common commitment to secure an ecologically sustainable future.

There is a relatively recent historical precedent for such a radical political realignment embracing people from all classes and parties. It happened during the Second World War with the formation of the Common Wealth movement in 1942.

Common Wealth was committed to left-wing socialism based on a strong appeal to collective solidarity and personal morality and conscience. It was established specifically to break the wartime electoral truce which had been jointly agreed by the Conservative, Liberal, Labour and Communist parties – the latter two parties having suspended the struggle for socialism for the duration of the war.

In contrast, faced with the threat of fascism (which was clearly against the interests of the overwhelming majority of the British people) Common Wealth mobilised mass support throughout all sections of society to fight, with equal vigour, the enemy abroad and the enemy at home. The enemy at home was that section of the establishment who put the preservation of their own wealth and power before the defeat of Nazism. Common Wealth's strategy was simultaneously to fight against fascism and for socialism by linking popular participation in the war effort with demands for radical policies to remedy social injustice.

The new movement's membership comprised people from all three left-of-centre parties – radicalised Liberals, left-wing members of the Labour Party, and non-dogmatic

Communists. Amongst its prominent leaders were Richard Acland, the former Liberal MP, and the veteran Communist and ex-International Brigadier, Tom Wintringham.

From 1942, Common Wealth put forward what, at the time, was an almost revolutionary political programme, including the common ownership of industry and wealth, freedom for the colonies, workers' councils in industry, enhanced civil liberties, immediate implementation of social welfare reforms, and the demand for a 'People's War' against fascism involving support for guerrilla resistance and armed revolution in Nazi-occupied Europe.

On this electoral programme, probably the most radical proposed by any party this century, Common Wealth ruptured the existing political constellations and provoked a radical realignment of British politics. Whilst drawing the bulk of its support from the working classes and the left, Common Wealth nevertheless also attracted the backing of many people from other class and party backgrounds. What united them all was the recognition that the mortal threat of fascism required a fundamental reordering of political priorities and policies.

It was on this basis that Common Wealth won a string of sensational by-election victories which, in some instances, involved the overturning of rock-solid Conservative seats – a testament to the scale on which the new movement had succeeded in winning the hearts and minds of former Conservative voters for a radical socialist agenda.

Though a wartime situation is obviously quite exceptional, the Common Wealth experience does point to the possibility that the all-encompassing threat posed by the ecological crisis could also be the basis for a radical political realignment.

To avoid the twin disasters of environmental ruination and resource scarcity requires a realignment based on the revolutionisation of our whole social order. It necessitates a direct challenge to the capitalist precepts of the private ownership of industry and wealth, production for profit, and the free market economy.

Under private ownership, industry functions primarily to

serve the interests of a privileged minority, rather than fulfil-
ling the needs of the majority and operating for the welfare of
all. With production for profit, the ecological and social costs
of industry are rendered entirely subservient and the consequences for future generations are largely ignored. In a competi-
tive free market system, industry is driven to seek ever greater
output, sales and profits, tending to militate against the conservation of finite resources and the nurturing of the environment.
The capitalist mode of production and exchange is thus a large
part of the ecological problem.

Contrary to the pure green critique, the ecological wasteland
which is springing up all around us is not the result of abstract
industrialisation, but the outcome of a very concrete and
specifically *capitalist* form of industrial development which –
harnessed together with imperialism – has literally devoured
the natural world and driven our whole planet to the precipice
of ecocide within the space of little more than two hundred
years.

In this period, which is a mere twinkling of the eye by comparison to the twenty-thousand year span of human civilisation, even those societies which have attempted to chart a
socialist course of development have embraced uncritically, if
not enthusiastically, many of the imperatives of capitalist
industrialisation.

Obsessed with the issue of the *state ownership* of industry,
state socialism has assumed that technology and industrial
processes are somehow neutral and independent of social systems, rather than being conditioned by them.

At the height of the Bolshevik power in Russia, even a fer-
vent and in many ways far-sighted revolutionary like Lenin
defined socialism as 'Soviets plus electrification' urging the
adoption of the American industrial management system of
'Taylorism'. It was as if he saw socialism as the state takeover
of existing capitalist technology in the belief that this same
technology could then be wielded in the interests of the working classes.

The inheritors of this Soviet socialist tradition, who see
technology as being ideologically free and above the class

struggle, have taken on board the capitalist-derived impulse for relentless economic expansion and the remorseless exploitation of nature for working class people throughout Eastern Europe. Large-scale discharges of toxic industrial wastes are causing the mass poisoning of rivers and forests, increased cancers and respiratory illnesses, and a declining life expectancy in the regions around the vast heavy engineering complexes such as those at Krakow in Poland, and in North Bohemia in Czechoslovakia.

The quest for ecological sustainability therefore requires the equal rejection of capitalist systems of economy and their proto-socialist derivations. Neither is capable of safeguarding adequately the environment, nor of husbanding the Earth's resources wisely.

The prerequisite for ecological sustainability is a green-rooted socialist economy where industry is under common ownership and popular control, and where, unlike Eastern Europe, industry functions on the basis of an all-embracing green consciousness and ecological planning which is specifically designed to counteract the fouling of the environment and the decline of global resources. In other words, politics must dominate economics, and planned green political priorities must become a determinant of economic development in a way which is impossible under a capitalist system. where profit-making and the free market are the overwhelming economic driving forces.

It is only when there is a high degree of common ownership and state economic intervention to control industry and constrain market forces that ecological objectives can effectively imposed upon the production process. Ecological Codes of Conduct, Energy-Efficiency Targets, Pollution Surcharges and Conservation Tax-Relief self-evidently work best in societies where the economic ethos emphasises social responsibility and human need, rather than self-interest, competitiveness and private profiteering.

A green socialist economy is not only necessary on a national scale, but also on an international level. To deal with the global ecological crisis, what is required is the establishment of new supra-national agencies under the auspices of the United Nations. They are necessary to ensure – in the interest of all peoples and all nations – the *planned* economic management of the Earth's resources, the protection of the environment, the more efficient use of raw materials, and the fairer distribution of resources both between nations and between classes within nations.

The UN Law of the Sea Conference in the 1970s provides a useful model for a New International Economic and Ecological Order. Though eventually vetoed by the superpowers, a majority of the countries involved proposed that a representative and accountable trans-national agency should steward, on behalf of all humanity, the Earth's maritime environment and resources which lie beyond the two-hundred mile oceanic exclusive economic zones granted to individual nation states. This agency should not function, they recommended, according to the unfettered capitalist criterion of profit and the free market. Instead, it should be based on the planned use and conservation of deep-sea resources for the common good of the world's people and for the benefit of generations yet to come.

The recognition of the intrinsically anti-capitalist and pro-socialist implications of a truly green political agenda has monumental significance for the creation of a new left-of-centre radical consensus and political realignment around the principle of ecological sustainability. It points to the potential contiguity and convergence of the green and socialist traditions as the focal point around which a new radical green political bloc might be constructed.

This bloc, encompassing progressive radicals of all persuasions and traditions, could be the basis for the ideological reinvigoration and reinspiration of what is generally termed 'the left'.

For the last few years, the left has suffered from a crisis of ideas and a paralysis of vision. Everywhere it has been in decline and on the defensive, unable to present an effective opposition or an imaginative alternative to Thatcherism.

A new radical green *and* socialist agenda might be the key to the emergence of a far larger and broader-based left-wing movement with renewed contemporary relevance and popular appeal. It could simultaneously thwart the danger of ecological catastrophe and offer a truly powerful challenge to the hegemony of conservative ideas.

This will not come to pass, however, unless there is the will and the effort to put these policies into effect. This requires a new-found sense of trust, respect and tolerance between radical liberals, greens and socialists, including a readiness to acknowledge each other's strengths as well as weaknesses. Liberals and greens need to recognise the ecologically-antithetical nature of capitalism, and socialists have to come to terms with the ecological inadequacy of orthodox left-wing economics.

Out of these new understandings, perhaps a realigned and revitalised radical movement inspired by green and socialist ideas, can begin to evolve and lead our society in the direction of a truly humane and ecologically sustainable future.

We Are All Connected

Meg Beresford

Arthur Miller's autobiography ends with the words: 'The truth, the first truth, probably is that we are all connected, watching one another. Even the trees.' Arthur Miller encapsulates my theme precisely.

My thoughts come from two directions: first from my involvement with the peace movement, of which CND is a part, and second from the fact that I am a countryperson, stranded unwillingly in the city. In my life and work I have to start by trying to achieve a degree of inner peace, a peace which I can then seek in the organisations to which I belong, and then take it from there to the world outside. In the first twenty-five years of my life, spent on farms in remote areas, I have developed a love of the countryside, wild places and nature.

I seek my values from these two converging viewpoints, and stress the need to keep a balance between personal, community and local interests and the demands coming from region, nation and the world. Just as it is simple to recognise the need for inner peace but extraordinarily difficult to achieve it, so it is easier to identify what is wrong with the world than it is to find answers. Solutions to global problems will not be found if we ignore the interconnectedness of all life – ourselves and the creatures and plants with whom we share the earth, and with whom we are increasingly losing touch. Gordon Zahn put it in a vivid way when he wrote that 'Auschwitz and Hiroshima fuse into common proof of the dehumanisation of man – who exhibits a profound sense of alienation and a distancing of responsibility for actions and decisions.'

Our modern world is all too often seen and experienced through the media, particularly television. Each day we are presented with a saturated solution of horror, disaster, war and strife encapsulated on the screen. We are removed from events and people as they are cropped down and fitted into two-minute time slots. Even the forecasting of the weather in this temperate country is presented with a sense of drama to people sheltered from it in centrally heated homes.

Only very occasionally does it really touch us. Michael Buerk's broadcasts from the famine in Ethiopia were exceptional. His words, spoken softly but with great feeling, combined with pictures of extreme human suffering to awaken our response. It was a human response: people gave, no questions asked – but it was not political. Politicians talked around the problem, pleading greater knowledge of the facts and thus justifying their failure to act, either with first aid or with ways of dealing with the underlying cause. It was notable that the political left had nothing to say about Bob Geldof, Band Aid or the Live Aid phenomenon. Charity in the biblical sense is outside their remit.

Because the world is presented through the media, and the media exists to entertain and provide novelty, we are able to switch off from a subject when the advertisements come on, when it becomes yesterday's news – and then the giving dries up. In 1987 Geldof went back to Ethiopia: there in the sun dried plains the refugee camps remain, people starve and die, the war continues, nothing is solved. Similarly, nuclear weapons and defence were news in the early eighties; now weariness has set in. The arms race continues nevertheless.

As city dwellers we are divorced from nature in our everyday lives. Nature comes translated into food in pre-packed containers. Chickens and turkeys, probably reared in battery conditions, appear on supermarket shelves encased in plastic and deep frozen. Flowers and exotic plants from greenhouses grace glass-and-concrete office blocks. In the parks every blade of grass has been walked over many times before.

We also have our human battery houses: the bed and breakfast establishments, the scandal of inner city housing policies starved of funds by central government. Whole families are crammed into one room to eat, sleep, make love – in a degrading half-life. When chickens are overcrowded they peck out each other's feathers and refuse to lay. What kind of adults will emerge from children stunted and confined in similarly stressful conditions? Meanwhile, at the other end of the scale, Members of Parliament attempt to seek rational decisions in a human ant-heap of overcrowded offices working inhuman hours. As Thomas Merton said, in a city like London 'The completely irreligious mind – the unreal mind, the tense, the void, the abstracted mind does not even see the things that grow out of the Earth or feel glad about them: it knows the world only through figures, prices and statistics.'

In terms of military spending, national budgets and the international debt crisis, prices, figures and statistics have become so enormous that they are meaningless and incomprehensible. The 1985 global military spending was well in excess of $900 billion – in human terms this is more than the entire total income of the poorest half of humanity, and almost $1000 for every one of the world's one billion poorest. Such sums are just as incomprehensible as the 'need' for the sixty thousand nuclear weapons which make up the global arsenal.

It is unreal minds that promote military technology, its targets and its rationale. They first have to identify the enemy – currently the Soviet Union, though this changes over time and with circumstances. There are also sub-enemies, Nicaragua and the Cubans in Angola, communists anywhere, the enemy within. We forget that 'the enemy' is as human as we are, calling him names – gooks, reds, commies, the 'evil empire' – because as Patrick Blackett, President of the Royal Society, reminds us, 'Once a nation bases its security on an absolute weapon such as the atom bomb, it becomes psychologically necessary to believe in an absolute enemy.'

The enemy, of course, reciprocates. The technological developments – blanket bombing of cities in World War Two and pilotless guided computerised missiles like cruise – mean that we are totally removed from any human contact with our target or our victims. If people come face to face with their enemy, look into their eyes, and see their blood, they may, like one American soldier in Vietnam, feel 'sorry, but I don't know why I felt sorry. John Wayne never felt sorry.'

The 'enemy' from which we have to be protected by suicidal instruments of mass destruction has frozen us in a bipolar competing world. It is set in permafrost, though it has melted slightly since Gorbachov came to power, and if he is given the space it will continue to melt. The permafrost is not an inevitable blight of nature, and it can be undone by human endeavour. We must, as Thomas Merton said, remember that 'History is ours to make: now above all we must try to recover our freedom, our moral autonomy, our capacity to control the forces that make our life or death in our society.'

We have to seize the chance to make history because our survival depends on it. Nuclear weapons could cost us the earth. In pounds, dollars or roubles we cannot afford it, not to mention the environmental and spiritual costs. So far Gorbachov is the only world leader in the nuclear club who has recognised that his country has needs which will never be met if weapons development continues to expand. Others, like the late Olof Palme and the leaders of the six nations which joined together to make the Five Continents Peace Initiative (Sweden, Greece, India, Tanzania, Mexico and Argentina), have recognised the peril and made practical suggestions for change. But demands for sanity from non-aligned, non-nuclear countries cut little ice. Environmentally, there is the constant danger of an accident. Spiritually, we suffer from a lack of moral certitude that the idea of using such weapons is quite simply wrong. Moreover, the quality of life under the threat, the dull fear pushed to the back of the mind that affects us all, is spiritually degrading.

We must promote what we are for rather than what we are against. We need positive alternatives and values that seek a vision for the future in which there is peace with justice, human rights and freedom for all; a future in which the helpless are cared for and respected, the hungry fed, and real need met with appropriate resources. This is a far cry from Britain in the 1980s, and the tragedy is that even the progressive and principled often begin to take on, albeit subliminally, the ethos of the present government's values.

Initially, anti-cruise campaigning was generated by a mixture of fear and anger: the fear of nuclear war; the destruction of our lives; the anger that authorities in Brussels, Washington and London, over whom we had no control, were introducing these weapons allegedly for our protection. No questions were asked of us, no consultation made with us.

The scale and the horrors of five thousand Hiroshimas makes the mind go blank. It is unimaginable, and the natural reaction is to shut it out. The unimaginable produces inertia, the same kind of inertia as amongst the people who Thoreau saw to be 'in opinion opposed to slavery and to the war, who yet in effect do nothing to put an end to them . . . they hesitate, and they regret, and sometimes they petition, but they do nothing in earnest and with effect. They wait, well disposed for others to remedy the evil, that they may no longer have it to regret.' As Thomas Merton puts it, we 'allow governments to pour more and more billions into weapons that almost immediately become obsolete, thereby necessitating more billions for newer and bigger weapons. This is one of the most colossal injustices in the long history of man. While we are doing this two-thirds of the world are starving or living in conditions of subhuman destitution.'

Starvation and destruction are the norm for many in the developing world. Even here in comparatively wealthy Britain many have poor housing, bad diets and inadequate health care; schools are short of basic materials and our inner cities are crumbling. Around one-third of the population – the old, the unemployed and the poorly paid – suffer degradation in the midst of plenty. I remember walking past the rows of cardboard box homes beneath the Queen Elizabeth Hall the day Fergie and Prince Andrew were married, the contrast of poverty and wealth starkly visible. And yet we continue to pour millions of pounds into defence – three million pounds a day for the next ten years on Trident alone – while ignoring the needs in our midst.

To achieve a future based on positive values we need to think holistically, remembering all the parts which make up our national life. We need to think globally, yet act locally on a human scale, taking into account the effects of decisions made at a distance. Government decrees on a wide range of issues too often forget or ignore the local effects of their decisions, decisions which impair the quality of life of the community and the individuals living within it. It may make economic sense to close small village schols or cut uneconomic bus services, but these savings ignore the stress on children having to travel long distances to school, and the loss to the community. Lack of an adequate bus service affects the older, poorer people who cannot afford or are no longer able to drive a car. These factors are not taken into the balance because they do not have financial worth. The long-lasting dangers of building pressurised water reactors or nuclear reprocessing plants at Sizewell, Dounreay or Hinkley Point are also ignored. The values which we are set in the balance must take account of the potential environmental, ecological and social impact, and be weighed equally with the economic and political.

It is difficult to strike the right balance, as was recently admitted by Michael Heseltine when he expressed 'a grave and growing anxiety in the South of England about the self-evident ravages that the pace of development there is causing.' Cynically, one might observe that he has only spoken out in his own and his constituents' interests, but whatever his motives, Heseltine is right. Within London and the South-East of England we suffer increasingly from stress and alienation. New developments eating into the Green Belt will exacerbate these problems, and it will become even less possible to find solitude or be in touch with the natural world. Lacking these escapes we shall die spiritually, being unable to find inner peace or tranquillity.

The peace movement has sometimes been accused of Eurocentrism by anti-nuclear campaigners in the Third World. It is true that our attentions have often been concentrated on local interests – Cruise at Greenham, the prospect of war in Europe. But the criticism is not wholly justified. The Greenham Common Women's Peace Camp in particular deserves credit for expanding the horizons of our concern. Making links between their situation, the victims of nuclear testing in the Pacific, and the plight of aboriginal peoples in Australia and the United States extends way beyond their own part in the nuclear tragedy. Closer to home, the peace campers linked their struggle to that of the miners during the long strike of 1984, sharing aims, tactics and experience. Moreover, Greenham has inspired peace camps at bases in Australia (Pine Gap), in the United States (Seneca Falls), and in the Cruise deployment countries in Western Europe. They have thus helped to create an alternative network of shared ideas and values across the globe.

Yet the campaign against Cruise took off as it did precisely because it was a local issue. Words like 'eerie' and 'frightening' are used by people seeing Cruise for the first time, and the overwhelming emotion is anger. It is much harder to generate the same sense of urgency about Trident, SDI and nuclear weapons testing, simply because they are so far away in time and distance. We need imaginative linking with other movements to bring the unimaginable to life in human terms. Greenpeace's courageous exploits frequently achieve this immediacy, indeed the sinking of the *Rainbow Warrior* not only alerted the world to French testing, but also showed their contempt for the law and the sanctity of life, and the length to which nuclear weapons states are prepared to go to protect their addiction.

Because of British official secrecy, it is difficult to ascertain the truth. We are up against bias and disinterest in the media, the vested interests of the arms industry and the military, and pro-bomb politicians sheltering behind official secrecy and over forty years of a cold war which has softened the public into acceptance of the status quo. Many people do have a genuine belief that nuclear weapons keep the peace, but in the main the public is ostrich-like, raising its head temporarily to gaze worried but uncomprehending on a disaster like Chernobyl (which 'couldn't happen here'), or stare with distaste at demonstrators parading in the streets. But the threat overshadows all of us, and many of these same people have a vague sense of unease. They feel powerless, or that it is all too complicated and better left to the politicians. But these matters are too important to leave to the politicians; as President Eisenhower once said in a speech alerting people to the power of the military industrial complex: 'We should take nothing for granted. Only an alert and knowledgeable citizenry can compel the proper meshing of the huge industrial and military machinery of defence without peaceful methods, and goals so that security and liberty may prosper together.' In the climate of the late 1980s our security is fragile and our liberty questionable.

Decisions on new weapons systems which affect all of us are taken at NATO meetings, and agreed without either parliamentary debate or public knowledge. The public is not told, and parliament is not informed until after the decisions are made. At Montebello in 1983 it was decided to develop a new stand-off missile system: British Aerospace started work on it in 1985. Yet as Scilla Maclean reported in the Guardian: 'Parliament has been told again and again that no decisions were made at Montebello.' Costings were not disclosed; the truth is not told. 'Five years later British MPs are suddenly to understand that work on British nuclear weapons, or weapons for which Britain is responsible, has not only been decided, but initiated and part completed, while Parliament has been told that nothing has even been decided.' The accurate information is freely available if you know where to look for it in the United States, and it has been debated in the Dutch Parliament.

The environmental and peace movements and those who share green and liberal values have clear areas of common concern. From an anti-nuclear perspective, the links are very clear. The nuclear arms race, the testing of nuclear weapons, the bombing of Hiroshima – all have far-reaching environmental hazards. If Hiroshima is forgotten or the test sites too far away, the fallout from the nuclear reactor at Chernobyl should remind us. The politics which allow the arms race to continue unchecked are utterly divorced from humanitarian values because of the threat of genocide. The sermon on the mount taught us that 'If a man looks at a woman with a lustful eye, he has already committed adultery with her in his heart.' By this standard, those who plan and secure the firepower to blast a whole nation into the stone age have already done it. Surely it is better to seek other means of solving conflict, using international co-operation and security.

When seeking values we can learn a great deal, both from other times and from other peoples, often considered less civilised and sophisticated than ourselves. In 1854, as the new territories spread westwards in the United States, waves of settlers moved into land which was thought to be empty and available. Native Americans whose traditional lands and hunting grounds were in the way were swept aside, losing everything in the clash of interest between competing values. Chief Seattle, a Native American chief, sent a message to the President which set out values most pertinent to our times: 'This we know. The Earth does not belong to man, man belongs to the Earth. This we know. All things are connected, like the blood that unites one family. All things are connected. Whatever befalls the Earth, befalls the sons of man. Man did not weave the web of life, he is merely a strand in it. Whatever he does to the web of life, he does to himself.' His message was not heard then and it is not heard now. The web of life, fragile and precious, which stretches across the globe and into the future, is threatened by people with power suffering from tunnel vision brought about by their narrow institutional interests.

Our horizons must expand from our small patch of the Earth to a Europe already divided by the superpowers, and out to the whole world. The military infrastructure of the superpowers is present in every corner of the globe. Many nations have it forced upon them, otherwise having no part nor interest in the ideological conflict between East and West. Only five nations have taken upon themselves the right to the monopoly of nuclear weapons, the signatories to the Non-Proliferation Treaty, who undertook 'to pursue negotiations in good faith on effective measures relating to the cessation of the arms race at an early date and to nuclear disarmament and on a treaty on complete and general disarmament under strict and effective international control.'

Except for the agreement in December 1987 between the USA and the USSR on Intermediate Nuclear Weapons, there has been complete failure in this obligation. Weapons are only removed as they become obsolete, and are then replaced with technologically modernised systems. The NPT was designed to lead to reductions in existing arsenals and to prevent the spread of nuclear weapons to new countries, but there are now six more nations, including Israel and South Africa, which have a nuclear capability, and a further twelve edging towards nuclear status. There is therefore the likelihood of horizontal proliferation as the monopoly of the first thirty years of the nuclear era is broken. In a sense this is understandable – if those who argue for the bomb within the existing nuclear powers feel them essential for their security and status, why should they be denied to the other 140 countries? Nuclear weapons for all is the result of this logic; thus it is argued that we have to keep ours in Britain in case an 'unreliable' country like Libya gets them.

With or without proliferation, no place is free from threat. If war should break out, the effects of a 'nuclear winter' would result in months of subzero temperatures and darkness in the northern hemisphere and a drastic cooling in the southern. This would dramatically affect the growth of plant and animal life, food crops as well as the surviving human populations. It is unlikely that a war between the superpowers started in Europe or the Middle East would remain limited, because military communications systems enmesh the Earth; submarines, armed and alert, lurk beneath the oceans. Even if deliberate war is avoided, accidents do happen. New and sophisticated systems can fail through aberraton, technical fault or simple human error; the twin accidents of Challenger and Chernobyl should illustrate the point. But the lessons are not learned.

Star wars and space based defence are on the agendas of both superpowers. The fact that SDI is a technological pipe dream – a hundred per cent effective defensive shield is impossible – is irrelevant. The research will lead to new kinds of military technology even if Reagan's dream is an illusion. The billions of dollars allotted for research and development are eagerly grabbed by weapons industries, university departments scratching for new funds, computer manufacturers and the scientific establishment – no matter that the money could be used to improve the quality of life for millions of people suffering from a lack of basic human needs.

This compartmentalised world means there are no adequate mechanisms for transferring resources from one budget to another, or for ensuring that basic needs are met, because those who are suffering lack the power to make their voices heard. In 1985, $2.5 billion a day was spent on military purposes. Such figures are unimaginable, but put into human terms, in the Third World dirty water used in households contributes to 80% of disease. Just $30 billion (10 days of military spending) could have provided clean water for all those in need. Adding another $1 billion to the $2 billion already spent could supply contraceptives to all women wishing to use birth control. Clean water and contraceptives – these we can all understand.

So far the 200,000 people killed by the bombing of Hiroshima and Nagasaki are the only victims of atomic weapons used in war. Rebuilt, they are now thriving modern cities, each with its own chilling memorial to August 6 and 9, 1945. Now, 43 years later, there are new victims: the survivors and their children who fall ill from radiation-induced disease – around two thousand in 1985. Even without war, there are many other casualties of the nuclear age. Tribal lands of native Americans and Australian Aborigines have been alienated and polluted as testing sites for bombs. Bikini Atoll was made uninhabitable after its use as a test site in 1957; the islanders were forcibly removed, tricked by their lack of understanding and given trinkets in compensation. They still wish to go home, but their homes are uninhabitable.

The French Security Services killed Fernando Pereira, a crew member of the *Rainbow Warrior*. Karen Silkwood was murdered for speaking out about the lack of safety in a nuclear power plant in Oklahoma. A crew of Japanese fishermen were caught in the Bikini fall-out. British and Australian servicemen watching tests with little protection are now developing cancers. Children are developing leukaemia because they are born near nuclear establishments. And wildlife is affected too, though this is rarely mentioned and never considered. As Robert Sheer, an observer to the US atom test on Christmas Island, said: 'And suddenly, I could see all these birds. I could see the birds I'd been watching for days before. They were now suddenly visible through the opaque visor of my helmet. And they were smoking. Their feathers were on fire . . . Instead there were just these smoking hideous contorted birds crashing into things. And then I could see the vapour rising from the inner lagoon as the surface of the water was heated by the intense flash.'

There can be no adequate memorial to the victims of the nuclear age, powerless people crushed in the interests of 'defence' and 'national security'. Chief Seattle's message must be heard. The nuclear industry in its twin guises of nuclear power and nuclear weapons is a major danger; the possibility of nuclear war is the most extreme indictment within our catalogue of failure to tend the earth.

It is undoubtedly easier to ignore what is happening than to act to stop it. We have become used to leaving such matters to the people we elect, assuming that they have the wisdom and knowledge to act in our best interests. But we should remember how often *they* have not made it their business to know, how often their judgment is wrong. Ultimately *we* are responsible for what is done in our name. Out inertia and lack of interest only allows for the continuation of many things we know to be wrong.

For too long we have accepted the expedience of nuclear deterrence knowing full well that it is cruel and wrong. Decisions made by NATO ministers gave us Cruise on our doorstep. It was decided in Paris to test bombs on remote Pacific Islands; in London to build a reprocessing plant in the far north of Scotland. Small scale, local, human considerations are swept aside as unimportant; short term expediency always wins out over long term cost.

In *A Fate Worse Than Debt* Susan George eloquently describes the vicious spiral of the debt crisis and multinational business interests in Third World countries. The IMF and the banks loan money to poor countries; the elites of those countries invest the money back into the banks in the lender countries, investing at the same time in prestigious industrial and military hardware. To pay their way, the Third World countries depend on raw materials and cash crop production. The prices for cash crops are fixed by multinational agribusiness and are frequently too low for profits to be made. Moreover, because of the emphasis on producing cash crops like sugar or coffee, the peasant population cannot produce sufficient food to feed themselves.

Modern farming methods, government and EEC subsidies, wage levels and inflated land prices have created an agricultural revolution. Former community enterprises – at harvest time, sheep shearing and potato picking – are now mechanised, and much of the closeness between the community and its land and nature is lost.

The cottages on the farm where I grew up, once homes to a dozen farm workers and their families, have been sold to townspeople for weekend homes. Pigsties and vegetable patches are gone, replaced by suburban gardens. The work of ten is now done by one with the help of machines. Farmworkers have died, or have been moved into old people's bungalows, and their children have moved to towns seeking work. To accommodate mechanisation, the shape and quality of the countryside has been altered out of all recognition. In the search for high agricultural yields and quick profit, must all forms of life suffer because their value cannot be measured economically?

The extinction of species is a fact of life. The present few million species are the modern survivors of all that have ever existed, but as *Our Common Future* says, 'Almost all past extinctions have occurred by natural processes, but today human activities are overwhelmingly the main causes.' The Brundtland Report argues the need to manage the ecosystem and to preserve species, as they may be used for resources in development and raw materials for medicines, as well as being saved for aesthetic and cultural reasons. Once again, economc uses will always win over the aesthetic and cultural unless we learn to respect and protect and preserve ecosystems, irrespective of their use.

In a just society, totalitarianism is resisted by the flowering of free spirit, the right to speak openly, the right to criticise and be different. In this country these rights are being eroded, and this tendency needs to be resisted. The better opponents of the peace movement admit that we serve a useful purpose in raising issues which lay dormant in the public's mind; the worst see nothing wrong in 'bugging and burgling' in order to prevent us from speaking out.

The early Quaker abolitionists opposed slavery not only for the sake of the enslaved black men and women, but also for the effect the institution of slavery had on the slave owners and slave traders. Only the very saintly are motivated by pure altruism. For the rest of us our own interests feature large in our concerns, but in this overspecialised and compartmentalised world we do not lift our eyes to see the whole. It is easier to keep our heads down and not notice, like the people who lived close to the gates of Auschwitz and got used to what was going on around them and failed to question the cause of the acrid smoke coming from the gas chambers.

I finished this chapter on the day that the 1988 budget was presented to the House of Commons. The Victorian values promoted by Thatcher's government have reached new heights, giving abundantly to those that have a great deal and taking away from those who have very little. A nurse doing responsible, caring life-and-death work earns less in a year than many financiers get in a week. My son, on a short-term community programme, earns less than someone at the top end of the scale will receive in his weekly tax cut. Within this ethos, success and value are measured in pure financial terms. It encourages greed and rampant materialism, and assumes that the poor could pull themselves up by the bootstraps if only they had the guts and ambition.

The same comparison can be made between rich and poor countries across the North/South divide. From the concentration on material success comes the need to protect one's wealth and property. It leads to the burglar alarm mentality, where new housing developments are defensive fortresses, built behind walls with dogs and guards at the gates, the previous inhabitants of the area having been priced out by 'market forces'. Nuclear weapons are but a burglar alarm writ large, one which threatens to blow us up together with those who might try to come and take what we already have.

For the sake of our health and wellbeing we need to turn our backs on the values of Thatcherism, and look instead to those promoted by the Sermon on the Mount. We need real values for all people, a future based on peace with justice, in which 'economy with the truth' is replaced by real truth and openness. We need a future in which we help our neighbours, especially those who are poor, sick or old, at home and abroad; in which we attempt to understand and know our enemies and to remember their humanity; in which we remember that we are not owners but tenants of the Earth; and in which we remember that we are all connected – even the trees.

The Environmental Crisis

Simon Hughes

'Treat the earth well. It was not given to you by your parents. It was loaned to you by your children.' One of the increasingly evident failings of our time is that we are relentlessly wasting the irreplaceable capital resources needed for our global survival. The international political order is driving us ever nearer to mass destruction. Either we have failed to understand our responsibilities or failed to execute them.

The theory can be put relatively simply. We are not the owners but the stewards of our world. We are all free to use it and have rights to enjoy it. None of us, however, has been given a right to ruin it for others of our generation or of future generations. An obligation of our international citizenship is that we preserve the freedom that we have without limiting the freedom of others. The precondition to responsible stewardship as we use and enjoy our environment is that the planet should continue to be characterised by diversity, both in its physical features and its resources. Our politics can only be consistent if individual liberties are not extended so far that they irresponsibly limit the range of environmental choices open to people in the future. To take perhaps the most obvious example, there are today reduced rights and choices for the half of the people of the world who live in relative and absolute poverty, and effectively none for the fifty thousand or more people who died yesterday because of lack of food.

The reality is that our global environment is being exploited, abused, despoiled and irreparably ravaged. There are, tragically, innumerable examples. To take one example: the introduction of the Nile perch to Lake Victoria in 1962 is now destroying Africa's largest lake, upon whose resources two hundred million people in Kenya, Tanzania and Uganda rely. The perch is eating to extinction Lake Victoria's four hundred fresh water species, and the lake is becoming barren such that even the perch may not be able to survive. As a result, algae are proliferating, the lake's life-giving oxygen is being depleted, and the ecosystem which relied on a species of native fish to destroy the snails which caused deadly liver disease has been disrupted, with fatal effects. To take another example: each day an area of tropical rain forest the size of the Isle of Wight is destroyed or degraded, deserts advance by thirty thousand hectares, two hundred million tonnes of topsoil are lost through erosion, and another species becomes extinct. Even now, a World Bank and EEC funded development programme in Brazil threatens the lives of thirteen thousand native people, as well as enormous environmental destruction. In our own country, we have since 1947 witnessed the destruction of 95% of lowland herbage hay meadows, 50% of lowland heaths and acidic soils, 45% of limestone pavements in the north of England, and over 30% of ancient lowland woodlands. At the same time, at the most parochial level and almost outside my window, one of the few remaining ecologically rich sites in urban London is being bulldozed, and is about to be built on.

Television and travel have opened the eyes of many of us to the vandalism and the danger of our post-industrial age. Whereas before there may have been an excuse that we hadn't seen and therefore didn't believe, now that we have seen the failure to believe and to respond is inexcusable. While the government has remained carelessly or defensively silent, it has been left to the heir to the throne to point out that over the next sixty years, if we go on as we are doing, something like a third of all the forms of life at present living on this planet may be extinct. He asked the most pertinent question: Can we feel anything but a kind of cosmic horror? It is not the responsibility of today's parents to try to ensure that future generations inherit a world which provides them with hope, fulfilment and wonder, rather than one which has been tested to destruction?

The requirement for anybody who claims that they are addressing the fundamental questions of politics is therefore to find the social and political, economic and technological pathway through the inner limits of basic human needs and the outer limits of the planet's physical resources. At the moment we are visibly failing.

And this challenge means another challenge, a challenge to established assumptions and views – about consumption, growth, nationalism, prosperity and wealth. It requires that we see things not just anthropomorphically but ecologically. It requires a redefinition of development. There is no excuse for not knowing where to start. The World Commission on Environment and Development, set up by the General Assembly of the United Nations in 1983 and chaired by the Prime Minister of Norway, Gro Harlem Brundtland, followed the report of the Brandt Commission in 1980 with its title *North-South: A Programme for Survival*, by setting out 'a global agenda for change'. The Brundtland Commission members were charged with working out a strategy for attaining 'sustainable development' for the year 2000 and beyond. It set out seven goals for the future: reviving economic growth; changing the quality of growth; meeting essential needs for jobs, food, energy, water and sanitation; ensuring a sustainable level of population; conserving and enhancing the resource pace; reorientating technology and managing risk; and merging environment and economics in decision-making. This is where the new politics must start.

We must look for the definition of success in quality of life not quantity of wealth. We must look for prosperity in ways which do not increase stress and selfishness. We must end the exploitation of finite resources in ways which deplete them more quickly than they can be replenished. From 1950–1980 the real per capita income in the industrialised countries rose by 6,000 dollars. Over the same period, for the eight hundred million people in the world's poorest countries it grew by a mere 80 dollars. We must correct the distortion of our use of resources where, a distortion by which we expend more on military research and development (one quarter of all research expenditure) than on energy, health, pollution-control and agriculture, and where in 1980 the per capita military expenditure in developing countries was nearly three times the per capita expenditure on health, while 44% of the world has no access to safe drinking water. If just eight hours of military spending, worth 680 million dollars, could be diverted, we might eradicate malaria from our planet and heal the two hundred million people who suffer from it worldwide.

We must end the disparity whereby roughly 95% of the total health research in the world is focused on the problems of industrialised countries. We must end the disparity whereby the rich countries of the north, which contain 25% of the population, consume about 80% of the resources. In Britain we eat on average three times as much, and consume forty times as much fossil fuel, as the average citizen in the Third World. In Indonesia, traces of pesticide banned in most of the developed world show up in mother's milk. In Hong Kong beaches are closed at the height of the summer because thousands of tonnes of untreated industrial waste are dumped into waters around the colony every day. In China air pollution in many big cities is so serious that many people have resorted to wearing face masks. Although environmental awareness increases, economic still rules. Malaysia, according to one spokesperson, 'has tried to adhere to international environmental standards', but since the economy was bad 'the government is trying to woo foreign investors by relaxing all kinds of regulations.'

Research, trade and aid all need to have their priorities reordered, and the criteria for judging success must be re-established first. As Prince Charles pointed out, the costs of action must in future be set against the costs of inaction. As Liberals have often argued, the change from our present society to a sustainable society will require a major change of attitude and practice, not least in our traditional approach to the economy. Conventional economics is overwhelmingly concerned with the very valid activities that are measured in money terms – the production, distribution and consumption of goods and services. But conventional economics has tended not to consider many other vital aspects of the human condition, both spiritual and material. Partly in consequence, policy makers have seen the gross national product as the overriding measure of human wellbeing. But in no sense if GNP a measure of the quality of life, not least because, in the long term, GNP takes no account of the depletion of non-renewable resources or of the welfare of future generations or of people in other countries. Our national profit and loss account will never be adequately presented by a chancellor who boasts, as he did this year, that our growth rate during the 1980s has been the highest of all major European economies, but who did not once mention environmental considerations. Wealth creation should in the future be seen as a means to an end, and not as an end in itself. Measures of national income and wealth should explicitly take into account changes in the natural resource base, health, and the contribution of the informal economy. We must improve the criteria for judging success, but we must also change the way we go about achieving it.

We must slow down both as a country and as a world; we must reduce our consumption of finite, non-renewable resources and give ourselves time to find renewable substitutes. Moderate fishing, for example, allows populations to breed and so allows the replacement of stocks; over-fishing converts renewable resource into an extinct one. Thrifty use of resources can have additional secondary benefits as well. Heat conservation measures not only improve the quality of life but can also reduce the use of nuclear and fossil fuels. In turn, this reduces the problems caused by radioactive waste and harmful emissions from fossil fuel power stations. The case for a change from a wasteful to a sustainable society is overwhelming.

We must establish ways of evaluating our priorities in such a way that integrates economics with environmental concerns, and always in such a way that evaluates environmental impact before any decision on expenditure is taken. Proposed legislation should have details of environmental implications as part of the preface to it, and structures set up to ensure that this process is properly carried out. Environmental scrutiny of legislation and executive action, together with accountability to parliament and to the public (always with open access to information), is a prerequisite for any move in the direction of a more sustainable economy.

We then need to ensure that financial and fiscal policy penalises pollution and encourages conservation. Tax incentives and tax reductions for environmentally acceptable activity must increasingly be developed, and taxation policy that ensures the most environmentally advantageous use of land and housing must be pursued. Subsidy should be given only when the subsidised activity is environmentally acceptable. Then we need to ensure that our legislation controls pollution and that our legislation and its enforcement prevents environmentally destructive practices. At home and in the context of European law we should seek to escape from the position of the 'dirty man of Europe' to a standard of pollution control that is the highest technically achievable. This applies to air pollution (particularly the emission of acid rain), to water pollution (both internally and offshore), and to soil pollution, whether by fertilizer, crop-spraying, or controlling runoff from industrial activities. The cost of preventing acid rain and the cost of a wholesale move to lead-free petrol and the effective control of vehicle emissions are miniscule compared to the environmental benefits. The danger to the ozone layer from aerosol sprays is now so widely known and so substantial that there should be early legislation to prevent continuing use of chlorofluorocarbons; CFC emissions need to be cut by 85% immediately just to maintain the current level of CFCs in the atmosphere. The UK has consistently opposed the stricter measures proposed, and although there has been some positive response on a voluntary basis by industry, both at home and abroad we should be acting speedily and effectively to prevent this remediable threat to health, to life expectancy, to the phytoplankton which is the primary food source of the ocean's ecosystems and to Antarctica, where huge climatic changes threaten to raise the temperature of the continent, which could at their worst – and most self-interestedly for us – submerge large parts of coastal cities like New York, Tokyo and London.

There also needs to be a fundamental change in our trading

practices. The developed world continues to dump toxic wastes, un-neutralised, in Third World countries, where there is weaker environmental protection. We continue to sell arms to developing countries who then spend three times as much on weaponry as on health care for their people. The economy of the West is sending goldminers at the rate of two hundred a day into the forests of the Amazon – after we have already destroyed 94% or six million of the native population in the 'discovery' of Amazonia by the 'civilised world' (tribal peoples now number only two hundred million people, just 4% of the population of our otherwise expanding world).

The economic crises in places like Ethiopia are caused by the First World, not the Third World. 99% of all deaths due to pesticide poisoning occur in developing countries, although only 20% of the pesticides are used in those places. For every dollar given by the West to famine-stricken countries in 1985, the West took back two dollars in debt repayment. The number of malnourished in Africa has gone up from eighty to one hundred million since 1980, with the result that a quarter of all children under five in sub-Saharan Africa are underfed. And all this has happened as the world's population has doubled in the last forty years, and is set to double again by the year 2010. Soil erosion in Ethiopia, resulting from the decline in forests from 25% to 3% of the surface area since 1940, has reduced domestic agricultural output by at least a million tonnes a year, which is equivalent to two-thirds of the food relief supplied. As somebody who has worked for the European Community, I am very conscious that the twelve are, by 1992, to be the largest trading block in the world; it is our responsibility that the terms on which we trade and the conditions of our aid are no longer so pitiful or so unfair. The percentage of our GNP which goes on overseas aid must be at least what the UN recommend – not half as much.

Where aid is concerned, it is not the quantity given which matters most but how it is given. We should try to ensure that it is made available to help people to help themselves. We live in a world where the richest quarter of the world's population consume nearly 80% of the world's annual resource production. Many of the resources that we consume are those produced in the Third World using labour, land and capital which should be used to produce goods that their own population need. As Mahatma Gandhi once said, 'The world has enough for each man's need, but not for each man's greed.'

I have hinted at the context in which these things must be changed. It is a context in which we understand that we are not an island nation sufficient unto ourself, whose own survival and self-interest must come first. Foreign, domestic and trade policy must no longer be based, as it is at the moment, solely on the principle of our own self-interest. Global responsibility must determine our national decisions, and partnership both internationally and continentally must be sought at every turn. Our national waste, for example, should be dumped where it is safe to all, not just safe to us.

The process of education, already started, must proceed apace. From the cradle to the desk there is a need for a fundamental reorientation of how we teach and what we teach in schools. Instead of nation-centred history, geography and culture, development education, environmental education, peace education and rights education must be taught to our children and young people, for they are citizens of the world. Destruction of the tropical rainforests becomes relevant if we point out that an area of virgin forest the size of Great Britain is irreparably damaged every year, and that every time we go to the chemist there is a one in four chance that we are buying something that originated in the tropical rain forest. Life-saving medicines, new varieties of food, timber supplies, all this vast potential and amazing variety are disappearing, possibly at the rate of a hundred species a day. These are tales of destruction that must be taught and must be understood.

This will inevitably have an effect on attitudes towards other things. It was President Eisenhower who said 'Every gun that is made, every warship launched, every rocket fired signifies, in the final sense, a theft from those who hunger and are not fed, those who are cold and not clothed.' The inter-relationship between us and others, between ecology and economics, between the international economic order and international defence, are clear for all to see. Our values, our priorities and our expenditure have been dangerously distorted; unless we correct this, we will continue on the path towards self-destruction.

The same principles apply at home as abroad. There is a need to educate people to limit the use of water if we are to prevent the destruction of further valleys for reservoirs. We need to defend the Green Belt and prevent poisons being sprayed in gardens up and down the land. We must teach the desirability of recycling paper, of banning lead weights for fishing, and of using the wind, the waves and the tides, organic waste and geothermal heat for energy, since we could easily meet at least one fifth of our energy needs from these resources. An agenda for change must be set, believed in and adhered to.

Our motto should be 'think globally, act locally', and this strategy should be equally understood by the intellectual and by the simple. The environmental audit should be as much a part of our assessment of our own standing as that of a government elected on our behalf. As the 1981 Global 2000 Report to the United States President put it, 'if present trends continue, the world in 2000 will be more crowded, more polluted, less stable ecologically and more vulnerable to disruption. Despite creating material output, the world's people will be poorer in many ways than they are today.'

The enduring values are clear for all those seeking to set and make progress for the new political agenda – environmentalism and internationalism, the redistribution of resources and an end to exploitation of them, a suitable economy, an understanding of our shared responsibility, and an opposition to politics and economics led by demand and appealing to self-interest. Hunger in a world of plenty is unacceptable, and rich citizens, including rich politicians, are at the moment living in an age of hunger. This must be changed. It is time for unity amongst all those many people who agree with Chief Seattle: 'This we know – the earth does not belong to man, man belongs to the earth. All things are connected like the blood which unites one family. Whatever befalls the earth befalls the sons of the earth. Man did not weave the web of life; he is merely a strand in it. Whatever he does to the web he does to himself.'

We are needed, in our thousands and in our tens of thousands, to change the direction of history in order to save our fellow citizens, our planet and our future.

Creating the New Economic Orthodoxy

Liz Crosbie

Since the Thatcherite revolution began in 1979, the political parameters within which all parties and social movements have been forced to operate have changed immeasurably. There is no longer any of the post-war consensus that previously served to produce some continuity irrespective of party 'in power'. The most obvious arena for conflict in the 1980s has been that of economics, and economic planning in particular. Even the use of the word 'planning' seems outmoded and redundant in the world of 'standing on your own two feet.'

Labour, together with the plethora of centre parties, has failed to critique authoritatively the principles on which this re-orientation has been based. Those collectively known as 'the left' have floundered due to a misunderstanding of the changing electorate and the long term implications for socialism of attempting to appeal on a materialist platform. This failure is especially marked when, by using the simple criteria of physical comfort for many voters, Mrs Thatcher's analysis wins hands down.

Empty rhetoric is no defence against a coherent analysis, however flawed, so if one is to engage in electoral politics for what remains of this century there remains little option but to revisit economic principles. We need to start again with basic assumptions, and from there develop a coherently reasoned vision for the electorate – hence this book and this contribution.

Whenever the high ground has been captured by an 'opposing force', it is necessary to develop a clear strategy for regaining pre-eminence. Although there are many with piecemeal plans to modify Thatcherite principles, there are few with a cogent and rational vision of an alternative Britain. Variations on the 'growth equals greater social justice' theme can be found in most political movements. True political success in the 1990s is, however, only to be achieved by asking the critical question – Why is the strategy of continued growth not creating a society which ordinary people wish to be part of? Why does the king have no clothes on?

There are fundamental problems wth the structure of our society, and to regenerate hope it is necessary to correct the cause of the malaise, not simply to cure the symptoms. Redesigning the king's wardrobe should be left to the illusionists, while those people of good faith who are not content with the prospect of a Thatcherite style government stretching into the twenty-first century engage in a process of re-evaluation regardless of political tribe or allegiance.

There are, however, certain core principles which we need to agree upon if there is to be a true dialogue. As a Green I would suggest that the basics are:

– a common understanding of the universal nature of the crisis, since narrow nationalism has no place in this analysis.
– a shared wish to see a non-coercive, democratic and enabling culture based on respect for the individual and on local variety.
– an appreciation that economic planning is a manifestation of a chosen culture, not the final arbiter of how people should be forced to live.
– a desire to allow diversity within the economic system, ensuring a mixed economy where scale is determined by appropriateness rather than by narrow cost expediency.

Working together on the basis of a minimum set of shared values does not guarantee that there will be harmony or total agreement on the policies to be adopted – the history of ideas demonstrates this conclusively. However, politicians are usually not intellectuals; those who choose the political path do so because their eyes are set on achievement rather than on maxims. When the future of our island and the very planet is at stake, adherence to political ideology cannot be justified. Let us allow political principle, but let us also bring open minds.

This is particularly important, since creating a new political analysis questions our own inner world and personal security as well as our intellectual understanding. Personal change and growth are often disruptive and upsetting, and when we review economics in the context of the twenty-first century it cannot remain a discipline which is removed and distant from our personal experience. The decisions to be made now are not just about how the 'government' allocates and uses resources, but how each of us engages in that process on a personal level.

If there is one seed of truth that has brought about the emerging analysis of economics known as green economics, it is an understanding of each individual's unique place within the overall economic system. There are many conventional economists who have outlined the benefits of economic development to the consumer/producer, yet it is only recently that the costs which are borne by each of us have also begun to be calculated. This process of re-evaluation is an essential part of green thinking of a holistic and rounded appreciation of the place of human beings in the natural world.

Limits to Greed

Green economics is based on the political belief that there is a fundamental parity between humankind and the natural world, for without the environment all human potential is negated. Respect for nature must be balanced by a respect for human integrity, every man, woman and child being born unique and important. To quote Christine Schumacher, 'The New Economics does not falsely seek affluence for the few at the expense of the many, nor the destruction of the environment which underpins all human activity.'

It is this balance between human need and the human impact on irreplaceable resources, a balance which we have so far failed to achieve, that must be the key dynamic in all discussions of economic planning as we approach the twenty-first century. The contribution which the new analysis will make to this debate is dependent upon decision-making being altered fundamentally so as to include the long-term implications of today's choices and decisions.

The see-sawing inherent in the two-party system must bear some of the blame for the shortsightedness so evident in successive UK governments. The problem, however, is worldwide. Integral to the ethics of commercial, business and political life in the Western world is the judgement that our own lifetime is the only timeframe worthy of consideration. Even the Japanese, who do accept longer pay-back periods, rarely incorporate wider costs and benefits into their accounting principles.

When the longer term nature of economic choice is taken into account, the simple truth that the natural world cannot continue to be pillaged indefinitely is so self-evident that one wonders why no one has taken it on board before now.

Until the advent of global war and instant communications it was possible to ignore the universal nature of human experience and human needs. When capitalism moved into the phase of providing sufficient wealth for First World producers to enjoy their leisure, attention also turned to the natural world as a realm to be explored and visited. Now many people in the privileged West are aware, through the media, of our global village, and we worry about the destruction of this garden of Eden.

As the dynamics of environmental degradation – including acid rain, famine and the destruction of the rainforests – are all too apparent, it is not necessary to catalogue in detail the symptoms of unrelenting growth. As our appreciation of the costs of economic development improves, questions about how to make possible a better quality of life for all the world's people are becoming focused.

The discrepancies between the First World and the rest are so painfully too clear to those who saw the TV coverage of Ethiopia, that econometric analysis is redundant in the face of the simple image of a tiny black child's dying hand dwarfed by a white rounded palm.

The dilemma of trying to provide for the world's human population can only be resolved by improved husbandry of nature's bounty. This view has been accused of being unrealistic, but the reality of providing for all of humankind demands the comprehensive appreciation of human potential, including all of the technological advances made this century. Green analysis does not want to turn the clock back to some golden age; it simply wishes to see the best of human endeavour addressing the core problem of providing for our basic needs without wrecking a world that we are only just beginning to understand. It is becoming ever clearer that untamed economic growth is spoiling its own nest, and that the notion of entropy is key to challenging the established orthodoxy of economic development. We cannot simply make the cake large enough for the disadvantaged to enjoy a share. We constantly see around us the costs of cleaning up or living with the by-products of growth, which have now reached the stage where the negatives all too obviously outweigh the positives.

Conventional economics has great problems in determining all the costs of economic growth, and only now are new criteria for development being devised. Green economics has designed tools to help us to assess our political aspirations and convert them into the balance sheets that conventional society requires. New indicators of economic development include:
– resource indicators and resource accounting, seeing the world as an asset to be wisely spent.
– a new indicator of national output, a reformed G.N.P., where all the negative social and environmental costs of production will be counted against the positive output, to give us a better idea of the real level of progress.
– an understanding of the human costs of that level of activity in terms of health and social cohesiveness.
– a wider picture, so that the informal economy is integrated into our understanding of development.

The challenge to the new style economist is to quantify and explain in accessible language the highly complex web of our lives, so that political decisions can be made with a better understanding of their consequences. The politicized economist must also grapple with the issue of how to remake our economy so that it functions sustainably, so that we can exist within the finite boundaries laid down by our environment.

North versus South

If green economics springs from the political commitment to the equal status of the natural world and human needs, then green international economic policy is based on an understanding that each human life is of equal worth.

Instead of parcelling the world's peoples into nation states lumbered with whatever resource allocation their territory happens to control, the Greens see humanity as a connected whole. Every woman, man and child should be entitled to dine at the world's table.

This entitlement is often assumed to be impracticable, in the belief that overpopulation is the root cause of the inequality. The notion that there are simply too many mouths 'over there' to feed is widespread, but erroneous. There are evidently areas of acute population pressure, but it is access to available resources that we should be questioning. The UK is a densely populated country with few natural resources beyond our soil and our remaining fossil fuel reserves, yet collectively and individually we use an enormous proportion of the world's natural wealth.

Are there any signs that the privileged of the world are prepared to change and let the remaining 90% join us at our overstocked table? One of the most significant 'consumer actions' of the 1980s was the way in which British people responded to the crisis in Ethiopia – regardless of whether one agrees with credit card charity or not, this was a substantial vote for helping our brothers and sisters in the Third World.

The emotional response generated by pictures of dying children is powerful, yet it can be debilitating. Once the first rush of sympathy has paid off, 'compassion fatigue' often sets in; the problem appears too big and too impersonal to understand. There is a retreat back into the private world that created the problems in the first place, the world of relative affluence. A more appropriate response is to change one's own behaviour, while at the same time motivating those who deal with the Third World on our behalf to change their attitudes.

The moral imperative for international social justice has sadly not been translated into tangible action by governments, multinationals and arms salesmen. There are far too many dollars, pounds and francs being spent on the pursuit of national interest. By the time debt repayments have taken their toll, the meagre monies filtering through to the Third World are simply not enough to challenge the increasing tide of deforestation, soil erosion, population growth, famine and war created by inequality.

The scale of the injustice suffered by the South cannot be rectified by the simple cancellation of debts, or by the payment of the aid ratios piously agreed at international conferences. To unite the two worlds of North and South demands a transference of economic power from us to them. The peaceful achievement of this transfer will demand moral courage and commitment from political leaders, but more importantly it will only be feasible when there is a full understanding by the general public of their role as active participants in the tragedy, and not simply as spectators.

Making the issues of Third World development relevant and clear to every member of our society will be vital work in the 1990s. Without a sense of integration and urgency, without making people feel that the changes going on are personally threatening, there will never be a suitable political moment for the structural changes required in this country to move towards a fairer world. Finding a route into hearts and minds of the British people will not be easy, but the reassessment of our position relative to the Third World cannot be kept at bay indefinitely. We all share the blame for our joint failure to feed the world on a planet which has sufficient resources.

Acting Locally

The deeply felt spiritual appreciation of nature implicit in much green thinking parallels a clear understanding that human society is our route to preserving the biosphere as well as being its enemy.

Because people are unlikely to spoil their own nest, except in exceptional circumstances, Greens see part of the solution to environmental decay in reconnecting human beings to their environment through a sense of appropriate scale.

Simply stated, if we live and work in close proximity, and if the environmental constraints are there before our eyes, we are better equipped to make rational decisions on how to use our own locality. It is this sense of rootedness that protects against the apparent human urge to make everything somebody else's problem, avoiding decision-making, and ignoring both social and economic costs.

It is the lack of appropriate scale inherent in modern industrialism that Greens challenge, not the technological processes themselves. Schumacher's idea of 'small is beautiful' has yet to be taken to heart, and the cult of giantism marches on. Conglomerates and bureaucracies aspire to continual expansion, producing a mangement process which removes from local areas the ability to control their own human and natural resources. The direct consequences of this attitude to local autonomy are omnipresent after nearly a decade of Thatcherite centralist policies. It is not simply towns and regions that are losing their autonomy. The economics of whole countries are enthralled to foreign institutions, regardless of the human or ecological consequences.

This powerful pull towads centralisation must be broken for local regeneration to take place. Economic guidelines should be redrafted to ensure that the locality controls both the wealth within its boundaries and the capacity to generate future wealth. Without this capability, all assistance to depressed or underdeveloped areas is bound to fail. Only when local progress can be self-generated through the creation of local wealth and the returns ploughed back into other initiatives, will real change take place and the regions be able to finance sustainable development.

This local 'power' is dependent on two key factors – the ability to generate capital from within, and the provision of the mechanisms to circulate resources internally. Both demand a level of local initiative impossible within the form of local government operating at present in the UK. Deep structural changes are required within government if rapid local progress is to be made possible.

When one considers the total failure of the regional support programmes of the last thirty years to alter the basic imbalance between the north and south of this country, the suggestion is not as ridiculous as it might seem at first. The potential benefits of a new approach to regional development in the UK would have substantial returns, especially given the new threat of overheating in the South East, distorting the national economy still further as the effects of economic overconcentration in London permeates through the rest of the country.

Local power is also about controlling the primary resource that defines most communities: land. Access to land ownership is crucial to economic independence, and most obviously in the Third World. The unfair distribution of land in many underdeveloped nations and the pressures of cash-cropping on the indigenous food supply are well known, and few thinking people today condone the denying of land to those who need it for subsistence. The problems of how land is used in the developed world are less obvious, and it is difficult to excite interest in this policy area.

Yet access to land and local control over how land in the community is utilised is vital to local economic evolution. As most of the land in this country is in the hands of a limited number of wealthy individuals and institutions, it is important that the needs of local communities can be met through harnessing these assets.

If the land is to be used sustainably and the locality is to enjoy a reasonable return on the community's assets, then the valuation of land should be recalculated. The introduction of a 'rent' from all land, to be returned to the community like the rates, would radically change the way in which land is managed. A rising scale of charges would provide an incentive to keep land close to its natural state, and the rent earned through change of use would be fed back into the community.

The path toward local regeneration involves many changes, but the basis of all these changes is the restructuring of economic power so that it moves from the centre towards the local community. At the root of this approach are the principles of appropriate scale, local control of resources, and the ability to create and circulate capital, which together will help to create sustainable communities, in turn fuelling the participation that true democracy depends upon.

A Green Nation State

Many green ideas began at the micro-level, and as the concepts develop, their significance at the macro-level is sometimes over-looked. The vacuum left by this lack of scaling up often divides potential supporters into two camps. There are those that see green thinking producing a massive build up of central power, with controls and coercion being adopted to ensure correct ecological solutions; and there are those who envisage the centre fading away organically as the regions increasingly look after themselves.

For any economy to be reorganised on green principles there will need to be a realistic balance between local initiative and national direction in the field of economic choice. The present inter-relatedness of the international community demands a coherent voice for delinking, and for the creation of new economic priorities. At the same time local power must be developed, strengthening the regions to generate the self-sufficiency which is the bedrock of a wholesome and ecologically sound local economy.

The role of the nation state in a green world will therefore be rather different from its present form. The government's funda-mental task would be to enable the regions to function autonomously through the skilful use of a range of methods of redistribution – both between parts of the country and between individuals within those societies.

The green state would also be the custodian of a revised national taxation and benefits system. All citizens would have a right to an income which would provide basic essentials, an income which would be paid for by a mixed taxation system including direct and indirect levies. The emphasis would be placed on taxing products and methods of production and marketing which created ecological or social strain by generating health risks or pollution.

There is intense debate as to how this alternative taxation system should be run in detail, and much more work is still required to quantify the potential monies available from pollution taxes over and above existing levels of personal allowances, mortgage tax relief, social security payments and pensions.

In addition to internal decisions about redistribution, a green government would be faced with economic decisions on the role of trade within its economy. Here in the UK we are obviously heavily dependent on trade, both visible and invisible, so refocusing the economy to be more self-reliant is a crucial task for any green government.

To begin with this will involve the phasing out of some of our most offensive exchanges – armaments and nuclear technology. At the same time, domestic production aimed at the local market will be encouraged at the local level. Current consumer trends towards product differentiation and quality will allow smaller scale business to grow up to compensate for the loss of long-distance trading.

The concept of appropriate technology does allow for large business units if the end products are desirable. Decisions about scale will be determined by including in the reckoning all the costs of a larger unit, including the stress resulting from wider distribution, higher communication costs, etc., and if the sums still add up to large production units, these can be accommodated within a green state. The crucial issues are how those units are controlled, and who makes the judgements about where they should be situated to minimize damage and risk.

Fortunately, the structural changes evident in the UK economy in the last twenty years have been accompanied by changes which suggest that a new kind of economy is evolving beyond traditional industrialism. This process is ongong, and demands a new kind of governmental support structure.

A green government will also need to manage our evolution

away from the centre of an empire by creating for ourselves a new role in the world which is not based on military or economic power over others. A sense of significance and security in other spheres is necessary if the electorate are to have the confidence to reduce spending on armaments and other technological fixes. Reviewing the global impact of the UK, by seeing it as a small part of a connected world, is our only defence against escalating economic commitment to a defence machine that is growing beyond our needs.

The striving for growth and dominance characterised by Western states is bound up with this lack of security. Not being content with what we have, the illusion that more will automatically be better drives us on, both as individuals and as nations. The role of a green government will be to reinforce an alternative vision, to show how impoverished our present view is, to show how it reduces our own country's prospects for true prosperity, and to remove the causes of our neighbours' envy, thus relieving their apparent need to threaten us.

This view may be seen to be élitist, suggesting that the poor must learn to live on what they have now or less. But it is the rich that must learn to live on less if this world is to survive. A green government should not strive to direct its citizens, but to encourage them through the use of incentives to change. The transition towards a sustainable future will take decades, but facing the economic choices that need to be met requires a commitment now to local production, to self-sufficiency where practicable, and to redistribution of resources to allow for a minimum standard of living for all and a sense of humility throughout the rich world.

The Buck Stops Here!

The value structure which green economics springs from is based on a firm belief in the role and place of the individual as an active participant with an enhanced sense of being part of a whole. The changes in the economic relationships within this country, and between us and the Third World, are only going to be possible if the 'dog eat dog' element of our culture can be minimized, rather than accentuated as it is at present.

This sense of connectedness is vital if we are to improve economic decision making, and if we are going to move away from faceless bureaucracies deciding for us to a future where we make our own decisions as to how our society should be run. For most people even being asked their opinion is threatening, and they feel totally unprepared to make decisions, preferring to leave it to 'the experts'.

Although most people know instinctively that the experts haven't got the answers, people have little confidence in their own abilities to make things happen. The scale of unemployment in this country is one example of an economic malfunctioning that is only going to be put right when people realise they must review the basic premise for themselves.

Nowhere does the empty rhetoric of the government minister sound less sincere than when promising to return to low unemployment. The post-war holy grail of full employment represents an ideal that most thinking people now see as impossible. By acknowledging the difficulties of recreating a society where 95% of the working age population have paid jobs, one opens the door to one of the greatest political problems of our age. Where will that paid work come from?

It is obvious there is a vast amount of work to be done – the houses that need repairing and insulating, the children and old people that need nurturing, the spare land that could be gardened, the rivers and lakes needing to be cleaned. Finding work is no problem, but it is modifying priorities to ensure that these needs are met that is the real dilemma. Only by rethinking what work means to us can we hope to find a way forward.

Not only do we not value certain kinds of work – the traditionally female or nurturing roles, but our society also fails to take account of the nature of much of the work that it currently views as significant. The theory of work to-day is lopsided, measuring output and productivity but not human costs and benefits.

Rethinking the nature of work will require active participation from the electorate if a sustainable form of economy is to evolve, and although incentives for change produced by a central government may help, the core of the shift must be a commitment to refute the politics of greed.

This commitment will be forthcoming only if the central myth that 'growth equals more for you' is shown to be false. To achieve this shift of thinking will demand political skills not yet seen in this century. Above all it will require an enormous increase in the understanding of conventional economics, so that it is seen to be based on a set of political principles rather than some god-given entity. For this to happen, the skills of the economist will need to be harnessed together with those of the social scientist and the communication expert to draw up a view of the economic process which people can easily understand. Without a widespread analysis of the cost-benefit equation that our choices involve, there will never be grass-roots pressure for change.

For a green economic future to evolve, structures will need to be created to facilitate and ecourage the individual to make more sustainable economic choices. Yet without a personal understanding of how each of us fits into the economic process, these structures are doomed to failure. For us to make the correct choices a much greater amount of information is required, and this is the greatest political challenge of our age.

Core Values

Any radical political vision presented to the electorate needs to contain the basic green principles of biocentric equality, the provision of basic human needs for all, and an understanding of ecological interconnectedness. These are absolute core values, but there are many interpretations as to how these concepts can be presented in the current political climate, and ways in which we might prioritise them. The Green Party has detailed policy for key areas of economic planning, but those who wish to identify a coordinated programme for change must understand the philosophical base. A piecemeal approach cannot be effective in reorientating the economy, and will clearly be seem to lack integrity.

The gauntlet is therefore thrown to which every group or individual can present these principles most effectively within the public domain. Unless the vision is discussed widely in informed debate, political life in this country is entering a very dark age.

Reclaiming the Politics of Emancipation

Hilary Wainwright

A plummy-voiced student called Georgina talked on Channel Four's *Comment* about how people 'no longer felt the state was theirs'. She went on to argue that 'instead of encouraging them to turn to the private sector we must introduce greater scope for participation into the public sector'. The words, the sentiments too, sounded strangely familiar. I remember such phrases as the talk of the radical left in the 1970s. Yet here they were, being uttered by a Conservative student in her bluest best, defending the government's proposals to bring market mechanisms into the education system. The words seemed stranger still when, addressing anyone defending local authority control, she said in effect, 'Don't worry dear fuddy duddies, loyal as you are to the old way of doing things, while all attempts at radical restructuring are painful, in the long run it's all to the good.'

It wasn't just that she made me feel old. I also felt assaulted, robbed of my hand luggage. She reminded me of how effectively Thatcher has hijacked much of the spirit of '68 and carried it off in an aeroplane going in quite the opposite direction.

While the emphasis may have varied, many of the political themes which developed out of the explosions of '68 were common to radical Liberals and the new breed of socialist. Both desired – though rarely specified – a participatory form of political power to replace both the corporate state of Western social democracy and the bureaucratic state of Eastern communism.

Both were internationalist, identifying with the struggles of the
Vietnamese and South African blacks and with new left movements across Europe. They turned their back on both the
British nationalism of Labour, and the cold war prejudices of
post war Liberalism.

Meanwhile, free-marketeers within the Conservative Party
were plotting their own revolution. They too were frustrated
by the existing institutions of government. For these Tories,
the problem was that post-war governments had raised popular expectations, and were unable to contain their growth,
expressed in trade union confidence and expanding demands
on public resources. Their determination to undermine these
social pressures on capital led them to the ideologues of the free
market; Thatcher turned the nostrums of these ideologues into
populist politics using the rhetoric of the times: the rhetoric
unleashed in 1968. The notion of liberation from state control
for instance, which became in her hands the liberation of free
enterprise from state regulation. Breaking down national
boundaries became a licence for the international movement of
capital. Creating the conditions for creativity and initiative
became objects of worship at the shrine of the entrepreneur.
Through these themes – expressed in vague general terms –
Thatcher built a broad alliance against the corporatist establishment and against Labour.

There was an element of inevitability about the right's hijack
of some of the emancipating rhetoric of 1968. They were under
pressure to innovate: the interests they represented needed an
ideological revolution to break trade union and public power.
After the humiliating defeat of 1974, there was increased
incentive and opportunity for the Tory right to take the initiative, and once the ideas were developed there was a responsive
band of newspaper editors and media pundits keen to fill the
popular vacuum on the right. But two questions need to be
answered before we can create the political resources with
which to regain the initiative.

The first question arises also from an international contrast:
why has the new left in Britain in contrast to say, that in West
Germany been unable to create any political alternative with

which to counter the influence of the right? In West Germany, for instance, the new left, through its social movements and its Green foothold within the political system, has had the effect of shifting political culture in an anti-militarist, ecological and feminist direction. It is not a shift which has huge momentum, but it has weakened the social power of the CDU government. Why has the dominant drift of political culture in Britain been almost entirely, though with significant local exceptions, in the opposite directions?

The second question is: how has Thatcher succeeded in establishing the most authoritarian 'regime', as she herself calls it, of any in post-war Britain and in contemporary Western Europe. That she could get away with it must surely point to a serious lacuna in the left's programme for the British state.

My argument in this essay is that one of the under-estimated conflicts influencing British politics during the last fifteen years has been the unequal combat between the freemarket right and the radical – and heterogeneous – left for the succession to social democracy. There are many factors making this combat uneven. But there is at least one which it is within the capacities of the radical left now, with the benefit of hindsight, to remedy. The new right and the new (post '68) left were both born out of the crisis of social democratic management of the state. But while the new right had a practical vision, however dishonest, of transformed relations between the state and society, the radical left did not. This is entirely explicable: the right was operating from above, using government, to undermine the diffuse, pre-political challenge from below. The new left on the other hand was shaped by the character of that challenge from below. Moreover, throughout the 1970's, access to political institutions for the radical left was blocked, by the leaden pillars of Labour.

Fundamental political change rarely originates from within political parties or from within the state – except perhaps when it is the outcome of war. More usually it is preceded by movements of a pre-political kind, questioning the values of the old order and prefiguring the values of the new. The French Revolution, for instance, was preceded by the enlightenment, in which artists, philosophers, scientists and the emerging class of entrepreneurs challenged – socially rather than politically – the legitimacy and rationality of feudalism. I would argue that the movements emerging directly and indirectly, from the turbulence of 1968 marked the chaotic beginnings of a new enlightenment, whose political future is uncertain.

By the late 60s, socialism of a sort that relied on government as the prime motor of change, had been tried. In the West social democracy had brought about improvements in working people's living standards and material conditions. This had also happened in the East, though at the expense of political and cultural freedom. In the West, better material conditions and education stimulated demands for participation in the control of economic and social life: students, auto workers, cultural workers and professional workers for the state all began to demand self-management as well as material satisfaction. Women and ethnic minorities, infected by this new desire for a deeper kind of democracy, increasingly demanded the democratisation of the personal and economic relations in which they were subordinate. For this, a change of government was not sufficient: they wanted emancipation.

In these ways the participants in the movements that spread from the events of '68 were groping towards a different kind of socialism. Some would spurn the label because of its negative historical associations. I believe, however, that it is still useful, in order to indicate the importance of socialising, in a variety of forms, the ownership and control of the means of production as a necessary though not a sufficient condition for the emancipation which these movements act. They started from their own situation. As a result, their experimentation focused on direct attempts to change relationships within society, but not political institutions. The emphasis was on using whatever social or economic power was available to achieve immediate change – in the universities, in the factories, in personal relations, in the media and other institutions of culture. Political parties seemed inappropriate to the kind of changes that these movements desired.

These attempts to change social relationships by awakening

those who acquiesce in them, rather than by crawling into political office, held out – in the 1970's – the main hope for social emancipation. To a large extent they still do. But even then, and even more so today, they needed political sustenance. By their very nature these movements have an ambiguous relationship to political parties. On the one hand, working as they are against the grain of dominant economic power relations, they need the support of parties with representatives in the political system. On the other hand, this has to be a form of political support which recognises the special transforming capacities of social movements, capacities which depend on their roots in pre-political forms of resistance and therefore their autonomy from political institutions. In Britain this kind of political support has been rare. There have been exceptions at a local level, for instance the Greater London Council and Manchester and Sheffield City Councils.

The relevance of this analysis of the social movements of the 70s for explaining – and then trying to undermine – Thatcher's sustained hegemony, is that in different ways these movements, including those within the unions, were trying to reorder the relations between the state and society. And what is equally important, they were doing so in response to a crisis of the social democratic state, a crisis indicated by escalating inflation, recurring and mounting strike action, and deep divisions within the Labour Party. It was a crisis produced by the limits of a social democractic state managing a capitalist society at a time of deepening recession.

These social movements were not simply pushing the burden of crisis off their shoulders. In their own spheres of society their struggles posed implicitly alternative relationships between political power and classes and groups in society in 1974–76. The shop stewards drawing up industrial strategies at Lucas Aerospace, British Leyland, Chrysler, Vickers and elsewhere were assuming, for example, a new kind of partnership in which an elected government would use its power to control or eliminate the arbitary power of private capital, while elected trade union representatives. Working with local communities and councils, would control the details of production.

The new women's movement too sought changes in social relations that were relatively independent of the political system, or which could not be changed by action from within that system. Its slogan 'the personal is political' directed attention, and action, to power within sexual relations and domestic life. The transformations which feminists seek, however, have lead us to see the need for change in the economy – for instance the organisation of working time – and in the state itself – in particular the control over social resources.

Meanwhile, the new right within the Conservative Party was also developing policies for re-ordering relations between the state and society. With Margaret Thatcher's victory in the 1974 leadership elections, their ideas did gain full political expression. They were well placed to benefit from the death throes of social democratic government between 1976 and 1979. Once the right were in a position of government – having got there without spelling out or perhaps even knowing their full programme – they then used the highly centralised powers of the British state to carry out their dismantling of the state's social provisions and controls.

Neither the Labour nor the SLD leaderships have any strategic alternatives. Their views on the relations between the state and society are moderate modifications of the status quo before Thatcher. They do not offer a real challenge to the Prime Ministerial powers which have enabled Thatcher to change so much with so little debate. In the case of the SLD, although it is radical on paper, it has to overcome a legacy of deferential parliamentary leadership eager to make it either in high society (Jeremy Thorpe) or in high politics (David Steel). The present leadership of the Labour Party does not even have radical proposals on paper. In their behaviour, for instance over Zircon and Gibraltar, they defer to Thatcher's use of the royal prerogative. The radical left on the other hand has no vested interest in the gentlemen's agreements and party patronage which protect Prime Ministerial power at Westminster. This much is made clear by the noticeably independent stands of Tony Benn, Ken Livingstone and others. The snag, however, is that these M.P.s appear isolated, lacking an organised popular base: preachers to ephemeral audiences rather than voices of a cumulative movement.

At first sight the main problem has been the absence of an independent party. Several leading figures on the left of the Labour Party had spoken out for social movements, particularly CND and trade union actions, in a way which does not weaken their autonomy. Inevitably, however, the issue has become the focus of internal party conflicts, and in the public presentation of the issue it is the party conflicts which are predominant. In Germany, by contrast, the social movements – though not so much the trade union movement – have the advantage of having in Die Grünen a party which gives them direct political expression. The Greens are now discovering that forming an electoral alliance and consolidating it into a party does not solve the problem, but at least it creates favourable circumstances for doing so.

The current impossibility of the radical left in Britain having its own independent party with national political representation presents special difficulties for challenging Thatcher's hegemony, but to rest the explanation of the left's weakness on this absence would be to attribute too much political significance to electoral independence. There are deeper ideological factors involved. If we look at left Labour support for social movements in the 70s, this limited attempt to break new political ground, potentially to reorder the relation between parliamentary representation and popular resistance, was deeply inhibited by the legacy passed on by Labour's institutions. Especially important were the assumptions about the working class and the state ingrained into these institutions.

There were – in the 1970s at least – two inhibiting factors in Labour's relations with the unions which had an influence on the left. First, the relationship is based on the assumption that trade unions represent workers as wage earners rather than as producers or providers or carers. The Labour Party is the party of wage earners, bargaining for a better deal. Its core ideology, labourism, is an ideology of decent and dignified subordination. Yet throughout the late 60s and 70s workplace trade unionists were taking all sorts of initiatives as producers, providers and organised citizens.

When in 1974–75 the better organised shop stewards' committees in manufacturing industry thought they had allies in government they put forward plans to democratise the nationalised industries – 'workers' control with management participation' as shipyard workers in Tyneside put it. Or, like the shope stewards at Lucas Aerospace and British Leyland, Alfred Herberts' Machine Tools, and the Post Office engineering department, they devised plans for social control over the design and uses of new technology.

Earlier in the 70s workers oranised work-ins rather than accept redundancies. Left Labour MPs certainly gave support to these initiatives. Tony Benn and the Institute for Workers' Control in particular tried to spread alternatives to capitalist management. At that time, however, there was not a strong enough base with roots in workers' struggles but with intellectual and political independence from labourism. The work of the IWC did not recover from the defeat of Tony Benn in the Department of Industry.

This lack of intellectual independence was reinforced by the structural dependence of the left of the Labour party on the established trade union leaderships, which until recently have often singlehandedly wielded the block vote. This has always cramped the Labour left from support for workplace trade union initiatives, which more often than not are frowned upon by the leadership. The result was that such initiatives remained isolated and sporadic. There could be no lasting and cumulative attempt to learn their lessons and develop a new kind of national and international industrial policy based on an alliance between elected government at all levels and democratically elected employees' representatives.

The second set of assumptions concern the state; most crucially the assumption that a Labour government will solve the problems. In order for this to have any validity, the priority of the left was to get a Labour government committed to socialism. Much follows from this assumption. Party policy making and conference resolutions are aimed mainly at laying down the basis of what Labour should do in government. The ideas that policy making might be about building on and generalising the ideas of a group of trade unionists with imaginative bargaining positions on new technology, or about extending the plans of health workers and users for more responsive health care, does not fall naturally within Labour party structures.

The result in the 1970s was that though left politicians would support all sorts of campaigns, rarely would they actually engage with these campaigning groups to learn and generalise from their attempts to transform the institution in which they worked, or which they used. On the other hand social movements frequently had what was in effect a split personality. In their own spheres they were immensely radical, but when it came to political institutions they often ended up lamely lobbying their M.P. Our ideas for transforming industrial and social life were not matched by an equivalent vision of political democracy. The result was that an opportunity was missed to develop on a wide, consensus-shifting scale. In virtually every service there were such groups of professionals and other workers, often in touch with users – teachers with parents, social workers with clients – all pressing against the bureaucratic character of the service and its automatic accommodation to financial pressures. None of these had any channel through which to make a lasting political impact and as a result they have tended to wither away.

Another problem with the left in the Labour Party in the 70s and early 80s was the complacent assumption that 'the movement' was their captive audience. Not until the mid-80s, particularly after the defeat of the miners' strike, did leading members of the left talk in terms of rebuilding the movement to reach new constituencies.

The relative success of Thatcherism has shaken many of the Labour left's traditional assumptions. The left in the constituency Labour Parties are more open than ever before to a political partnership with activists at the base of the unions, even if it does incur the wrath of trade union hierarchies. They are more responsive to the insights of social movements and popular initiatives. Their involvement in setting up the Socialist Conference in Chesterfield with organisations independent of the Labour Party is an indication of this openness to new thinking.

These developments are taking place, ironically, just at a time when many social movements are in decline – at least in their original mass form – and new ones are only tentatively discovering the appropriate form for the times. It will not be enough simply to try to pick up the threads of the 70s. It will require a far more conscious long-term effort to build a movement, to stimulate a broadly socialist enlightenment. Such a movement will need to connect two levels of agitation without losing the distinctiveness of each. One the one hand, it will need to reach out to spread and to support campaigns for transformation of the social and economic institutions of daily life. On the other hand, it will need to elbow its way into national debate – and increasingly, European, debate – with principles and proposals for political transformation. Such proposals should have as their aim the strengthening of the democratic capacities of parliament and the weakening of its role as a bulwark of the existing state. In my opinion this would require the elimination of all Royal Prerogatives, the subjection of matters of national security to parliamentary scrutiny, the creation of federal parliaments with powers to raise funds, and control regional economic development, the introduction of an electoral system of proportional representation, the democratisation of the judiciary and a constitution laying down political and social rights. These issues are only belatedly being debated on the left. There has been a false counter-position of these democratic reforms to the process of building extra-parliamentary movements. In fact the more democratic are parliamentary institutions the more directly they can reflect and support social movements organised outside conventional politics. The other side of this is that the more open, accessible and accountable parliamentary institutions, the less easily can the City speculator, corporate bosses and media magnates gain cover for sabotage of those who seek to challenge their power.

The term 'movement' no longer has much political force. The rhetoric of TIGMO (This Great Movement of Ours), spoken by people who have long since ceased to build it, has emptied it of the powerful meaning it has had in earlier years. The radical left needs to reclaim the idea of a movement as a powerful influence on national politics.

What is distinctive about a movement? First, its combination of diverse starting points and a common direction; of autonomous organisations supported by a common framework. Secondly, its primary base outside conventional party politics. This does not mean that it is unorganised, merely a spontaneous wave of social feeling. On the contrary, a movement aims to reach parts of society that political parties do not reach; to be successful, therefore, it has to be organised, and in an immensely creative and flexible manner. Its dynamism comes from the questioning and resistance to be found in people's daily lives long before it takes a political form. A movement for socialism needs the support of political parties, MPs and councillors, but its aim must be to build a movement in society, a movement which can demand and use party political support rather than simply be grateful that it was given.

Why is it so urgent to consolidate such a movement now?

First, to overcome the isolation of people's resistance and to ensure that the education and the confidence that they gain in the course of this resistance is not lost. The prospect of isolation is likely to grow as Thatcher's strengthening of market forces produces an increasingly dual society. There will be the isolation of those temporary and part-time workers who stand up for a decent livelihood – unions are willing to collect their subs but not always so keen to risk resources in supporting these workers' small unglamourous struggles.

Then there is the isolation of communities whose future is threatened by corporate de-investment or by property speculation, but whose existence is too far from Fleet Street to be noticed. Local councils are increasingly too absorbed in their own problems to provide the necessary support for community action to have an effect.

Finally, there is the isolation of individuals driven to breaking point. Thatcherism feeds on isolation like a vulture feeds on death.

Secondly, we are living in a period when even high profile political initiatives will only find an echo in society if a movement has prepared the way. The campaign against the privatisation of electricity or for the defence of left-wing local councils will depend on their effectiveness on a far wider movement for socialism in every city and town. The reason why our campaigns depend upon a broader cultural movement becomes apparent when we reflect on how the relative success of the left in the 60s and 70s depended in part on the tattered remnants of the social democratic consensus originating in the Labour government of 1945. Inadequate though we believe this consensus to be, it did provide a kind of protection while we moved beyond it. That consensus is now being destroyed, and if socialist politics are to thrive and grow we need to create a less patronising, less deferential, more participatory, more confident socialist culture.

Emphasising political culture does not mean that we ignore political power. It is rather that the kind of political transformations that socialism aims to bring about require far deeper changes in consciousness than anything electoral politics can bring about. It needs to achieve the kind of challenge to the legitimacy and rationality of capitalism that the Enlightenment made to the values and institutions of feudalism.

This is not as rhetorical as it may sound. In present circumstances, virtually every struggle or campaign contains more or less explicitly a moral challenge and an alternative set of values. The miners' strike, as well as being about the defence of jobs, was about challenging the legitimacy and rationality of de-investment decisions which laid whole communities to waste. The seafarers are striking against management strategies which put profit before health, safety and well-being. The kind of movement which needs to be built – in many ways *is* being built – must not only be able to provide more co-ordinated practical support for such disputes, but also to provide a means of making explicit and public the wider social and moral challenges which they contain.

The important realignment on the left which is now needed is not primarily within party politics but is in creating – or consolidating – movements which can reclaim the culture of emancipation from individualism. We will know we are getting somewhere when parents or teachers appear on the Channel Four *Comment* slot explaining their plans for educational democracy.

Towards a Green Europe and a Green World

Petra Kelly

I believe that the green way of thinking and living is here to stay, even if some of the green parties will not survive into the 1990s. I also believe that human beings are here to stay as long as we do not make compromises when it comes to questions of life and death.

We cannot have a little bit of cancer or a little bit of malnutrition, a little bit of death or a little bit of social injustice or a little bit of torture. Neither is there a little, more acceptable, bit of war, or a little bit of peace.

It does not help any of us in any way if we begin accepting lower, so-called 'safer' levels of radioactivity, lead and dioxin. We must speak out loudly and courageously if we know there to be no safe level. This must be our approach to achieving peace.

Decentralisation, global responsibility, developing a truly free and non-violent society in our own communities, showing solidarity across national boundaries and ideologies with people who are repressed and discriminated, practising civil disobedience against the nuclear and military state – all this can be done very effectively without making compromises all along the way until we reach a point of no return.

I believe that greens have much power already today, and I also believe we have much responsibility, and can work without compromising and joining any alliances, a topic that many European green parties have agonised over.

The recent turmoil in my own Green Party concerning the question of NATO membership and unilateral disarmament is troubling me, as are a whole range of other internal squabbles. From these troubles others can learn, and I can only plead with you not to repeat our mistakes.

It is a very, very sad thing, watching on the one hand how we can upset traditional voting patterns and traditional politicians on both right and left, achieving great electoral successes; then seeing how we can bring just as much disarray and upset upon ourselves.

The conflicts which the West German Greens have experienced have much to do with the clash of interests between those coming from a rather dogmatic, old, leftist political perspective which shares so many anti-capitalist insights, and those who come from a holistic New Age perspective whose aims I also very much support. The clash of interest is often not so much in what we are aiming for, but how we can get there and what strategies we should pursue towards our common goal.

There are those in our party, the 'Realos', who want to moderate our political programme so that we become more acceptable as political partners for the SPD. It is the 'Realos' who have even questioned our green strategy of unilateral disarmament, and our aim of dismantling the two military blocs, starting at home with NATO.

Then there are also the undogmatic, radical, independent ecologists and pacifists in the Greens, with whom I count myself. We hope to reconcile the differences I have described if the Green Party is to survive. We do not, however, want to moderate or soften the programme for the sake of cheap power tactics.

Ironically, the splits beng faced by many of Europe's green parties raise the same issues in microcosm that we must face in trying to achieve a green Europe and a green world. My colleagues, both in Germany and in other countries where greens have been successful in electoral terms, face the problems of how they react to established power blocs, and where and when to make compromises.

What has always given me hope is the fact that authentic green movements, action groups and parties have not been wedded to the old style ideologies. We were and still are genuinely open to new and radical nonviolent, feminist ecological and pacifist approaches.

We face the dilemma once phrased in the form 'whoever wants the world to remain as it does, does not want it to exist.' We face the paradox that Albert Einstein described, that the splitting of the atom has changed everything except the way people think. That is what we set out to do: to help change the way people across Europe and throughout the world think; to help people act locally and think globally.

In all our activities, but nowhere more importantly than with our actions for peace and greater co-existence, we must help people to see beyond their own needs and to see wholly. There is much controversy between the leftist political and holistic spiritual wings of the green movement, but it is important to see how both wings belong together, complement each other, are part of each other, because we cannot solve any political problems without also addressing the spiritual ones. Green politics has a spiritual basis which respects all living things and understands the interrelatedness and interconnectedness of all living things. This colours our whole approach, and defines all our political activities. The political is the personal, and the personal is the political.

Simply repairing the existing systems – whether they be capitalist or socialist – should not be our aim. Our aim is the nonviolent transformation of social structures. Our aim is radical, nonviolent change of a patriarchal society which has been militarised and become accustomed to the use of force.

We must make a complete break with both the concepts and mechanics of militarism. Unilateralism is more than a mechanical process of arms reduction, but a way in which greens can declare their independence to respect democratic decisions even when they conflict with the assumptions of the cold war, by refusing to submit to a bloc mentality. Unilateralist approaches to disarmament might be the first step in arms reduction, but they crucially also take the first step towards breaking down the existing systems that militarise society at every level.

Peace has a wider meaning for us. It is not just the absence of mass destruction, but a positive internal and external condition in which people are free so that they can grow to their full potential.

We can be successful if we truly believe in our own concept of power, a new type of power that is about abolishing power as we know it. Power over others must be replaced by shared power, by the power to do things, by the discovery of our own strength as opposed to being the passive recipients of power exercised by others, often in our name. From our own strength and the concept of the power of nonviolence, we can draw the vision of the green Europe and the green world that we seek.

An ecological society is a truly free society. This means searching for soft, decentralised technologies and energies, and for ways of true co-determination and self-determination. We reject and wish to move away from the monolithic technology and monolithic institutions of the military-industrial complex. A truly free society must also mean the guarantee of economic, social and individual human rights. It means that we must speak out loudly to be heard and counted wherever basic human rights are not respected, regardless of the country or ideology that violates human rights, whether Poland or Chile, South Africa or Turkey, the USA of the USSR.

'Glasnost' must recognise the right of each of us to practise 'detente from below'. There are many friends in independent green initiatives in East Germany, Hungary, Poland, the Soviet Union and Czechoslovakia who are missing from international gatherings of greens.

Women from five European countries where deployment of American or Soviet nuclear missiles had taken place said in their joint statement: 'We seek neither peace that suppresses us nor war that destroys us . . . Forty years after Auschwitz and Hiroshima, forty years after the start of confrontation between the blocs, we at long last want to start jointly to get to know and understand each other better and to meet across the wall that not only divides our states but all too often our minds and hearts as well. We have started detente at the bottom: join us.'

Green movements are growing daily within Eastern Europe as in the West, and we must never forget them. Nor can our thinking on these issues be Eurocentric; we must take action for the right of everyone to practise detente from below.

A truly free society means that we do not want peace which oppresses us. We must learn, in our own terms, what peace and freedom mean. The phrase 'peace and freedom' has been for too long part of the right-wing vocabulary and ideology, sadly neglected by the left and even by greens.' I have been disappointed to see the amount of time, effort and money some greens have put into campaigns against the Contras in Nicaragua, yet at the same time neglecting the question of Afghanistan or the question of political prisoners in the countries of Eastern Europe.

There can be no peace if there is social injustice and suppression of human rights, because internal and external peace are inseparable. When we try to rid the world of things as oppressive as nuclear, chemical and conventional weapons; poverty, sexism and racism, it can help us to look at their structural underpinning: the system of patriarchy which is found in all systems whether they be capitalistic or state socialistic.

Patriarchy is the system of male domination, prevalent in both capitalist and socialist countries, which is suppressive to women and restrictive to men. Patriarchy is a hierarchical system in which men have more value, more social and economic power, and under which women suffer both from oppressive structures and from individual men. It shows itself in all areas of our lives, affecting political and economic structures, our work, our homes, and our professional relationships.

To put it bluntly, men are at the centre of a patriarchal world in East and West, South and North. Yet I believe that norms of human behaviour can and do change over the centuries, and these aspects can be changed also. No pattern of domination is a necessary part of human nature.

The type of true disarmament we are talking about has been expressed by the women from the five countries. In their 'letter across the blocs' they said: 'Despite our differences, we are united by the will for self-determination, to struggle against the culture of militarism in the world, against the uniforms and violence, against our children being educated as soldiers, and against the senseless waste of resources. We demand the right of self-determination for all individuals and peoples. We want to make a specific cultural contribution to changing existing social structures. That is why we also challenge conventional gender roles and why we ask men to do the same. The freedom to determine one's own fate also means freedom of exploitation and violence: in our thoughts and actions, at our places of work, in our relationship with nature and the relationship between men and women, between generations, between states, between East and West, and between North and South in global terms.'

We must, I believe, hold on to our strategies of unilateral disarmament, always making the first step and never pointing at the other side before we look at our own glass house.

The public's mentality is shaped to a very great extent by the concept of deterrence and bloc-oriented thinking: NATO in our minds and souls, the Warsaw pact in the minds and souls of others. This is unfortunately the reality that we must come to terms with. But precisely for this reason, we must start here, with the question of the blocs and their conditioning, which results in the legitimisation of the arms buildup of each bloc. It is this stereotyping of each other as an enemy, following the logic of military blocs, that constitutes a deep-rooted barrier which we must learn to surmount.

For European greens, our policy must be one of military non-alignment. We must take the unilateral steps necessary to leave NATO; not just to dissolve that power bloc but to send the necessary signals to the Warsaw pact countries that they too could seek their own 'independence'. To embark on a departure from the whole military system is to initiate a policy of non-threatening conduct.

This policy can be styled as establishing 'common security' though it is more accurate when greens refer to it as 'breaking out of the logic of military bloc confrontation'. To do this, we must 'meddle' in the affairs of the other bloc as well as in those of our own. We are, as Martin Luther King stated, caught in a network of mutuality. We are tied in a single garment of destiny. Whatever affects one directly, affects us all indirectly.

We want to create now the conditions for a new way to peace that is more than just the absence of war. Our idea of social defence presents an alternative to the dead-end self destruction of the arms race. Social defence, defence by non-military means against a military attack from outside or within, is based on the idea that a society cannot be controlled if it is not prepared to co-operate with the oppressor. One of our most important tasks is to encourage the acceptance of such an attitude of social defence. Social defence depends upon actions to prevent the opposition from achieving their aims, which undermine its ability to fight and at the same time strengthen one's own ability to resist. Social defence can mean general strikes, boycotts, blockades, putting facilities that are important to the opponent out of action, influencing the occupying troops, and creating an efficient communication system of one's own. There are already many examples of peaceful resistance, nonviolence and civil disobedience in many locations in Germany.

Our policy of non-alignment and non-threatening conduct is not confined to Europe, but dovetails with the independence movements of the countries of the Third World, who until now have been kept in a state of underdevelopment and depen-dence. Growing non-alignment, wherever it occurs, improves the prospects for peace and freedom worldwide.

Practising detente from below across all national boundaries and ideologies is the most internationalist task for us all. This means that we should stay in touch with those high up in places of power, but at the same time we should devote our time and efforts to relating to those in political nonviolent opposition, to those working in independent initiatives who are still haras-sed and politically suppressed.

We have welcomed the trade union and civil rights move-ments in Eastern Europe, such as Solidarity in Poland and the Charter 77 Group in Czechoslovakia. We recognise in these movements the principles of social justice, basic democracy and nonviolence. They, too, are helping through detente from below to create a climate that welcomes disarmament.

Practising detente from below also means doing everything possible to build up a demilitarised, non-aligned Europe in the spirit of Olaf Palme, as opposed to the Western European military and nuclear superpower now in the making. We can see, reading between the lines, that conservative and reactionary forces in West Germany are in favour of British and French nuclear co-operation including, one day, German participation on the basis of full equality. The ideas put forward in the 1960s for a 'German finger on the nuclear trigger' are being commonly discussed again. I believe that one of the most important tasks for European greens is the prevention of a third military and nuclear superpower, called Western Europe.

In Duisberg in 1983, West German Greens adopted the declaration entitled *Dissolve the military bloc – leave NATO*, which included the following:

We are
– *in favour of nuclear-free zones and a nuclear free Europe;*
– *in favour of overcoming the spirit, logic and policy of deterrence;*
– *in favour of increasing the co-operation amongst peace and emancipation movements across all borders and blocs;*
– *in favour of steps of unilaeral disarmament being taken by all countries; we must start in our own country;*
– *in favour of the two military blocs, NATO and the Warsaw Pact, being dissolved; we must leave NATO;*
– *In favour of all foreign troops being withdrawn from West Germany and ultimately from all other countries as well;*
– *opposed to any arms build up by means of nuclear, biological, chemical or conventional weapons;*
– *opposed to any methods of directly or indirectly exporting weapons systems, military knowhow or means of suppression;*
– *opposed to any policy of direct or indirect intervention;*
– *opposed to any co-determination in the firing of nuclear weapons on West German soil;*
– *opposed to dumps of toxic, nuclear waste in the Federal Republic;*
– *in favour of strong promotion and effective organisation of*

conscientious objection as well as full implementation of the civil and trade union rights of persons doing substitute civilian service and of soldiers in the armed forces;
— in favour of the right to refuse both military and substitute civilian service;
— in favour of the promotion of peace research, instead of its curtailment;
— in favour of the development of concrete models of arms conversion;
— in favour of the development of concrete steps in the field of an alternative security policy aimed at social defence.

In this way we would achieve a peaceful, non-threatening West Germany, as a model for other European countries.

We reject thinking along the lines of the former British Prime Minister, James Callaghan. He recently demanded that the European 'pillar' of NATO be strengthened, saying: 'It is obvious that we weaken NATO if we present European and Atlantic co-operation as alternatives, as France did in the past ... It is completely wrong to argue that the reason for political and military co-operation among the Europeans is simply opposition to American policies because, after all, the interests of NATO are also at stake. The way in which we handle activities outside the NATO area could scarcely be worse. One possibility would be to set up a Euro-American group for consultations on conflicts outside the NATO area, this group existing alongside the official NATO structures. But the growth of European strength at a time when nuclear strategy is threatening to determine the relationship between the USA and the USSR enables us to develop Europe in the field of defence as well as in the economic, trade and political spheres into a strong second pillar if we choose to do so.' Callaghan makes it very clear that the 'Europeanisation' of Europe has nothing to do with new independence, sovereignty and autonomy for Europe, but instead leads to a second pillar to American and NATO interests.

We must do everything possible to begin, within our own

ranks, nonviolent conflict resolution and the spread of knowledge and training concerning social defence. We must be very clear about what we mean when we call ourselves a nonviolent party and a nonviolent movement. The means and the ends must be parallel. You cannot reach a peaceful end with violent means, and you cannot reach a just end with unjust means.

Last, but not least, we must in the process of bringing more peace and justice and harmony to this world become more peaceful and just and tolerant ourselves, with one another, within our own ranks. The small-hearted spirit and the attitude of not trusting and always controlling each other within my own Green Party has been a strong disappointment to many of us, and has done much to minimalise our appeal, our chances and our concrete results.

Participatory democracy must not become a new formula for demagoguery, for misuse of grass-roots power, for tactics. It does not mean hurting each other just because there is a disagreement. There must always be room for tolerance, for accepting each others' positions and points of view, just as there must always be room to act according to our own conscience.

In our own movement, as in the world, we must respect each individual, his and her talents and individuality – without coercion, without mistrust and without committees and bureaucracies to control and watch over them. Living our values is what green politics is all about, and by living them they cannot fail to become the values of our communities, then our nation and our continent, and then the new values of the world.

Through practising detente from below, we are challenging not only the moral authority but the practical ability of those who wish to make decisions on our behalf. Carl Rogers, of the Institute for Peace, California, has said that 'Many, many years from now, when the telling of history is told, people will hear about the 1980s. A fragile era where a hydra of tensions and conflicts threatened the survival of the planet – where terrorists menaced the innocent, racial and religious wars overtook great countries, and children became armed militia . . . The time was also marked by an uprising of the human spirit – founded on peoples' faith that within them was a vast reservoir of good. People knew . . . they could be trusted with Peace.'

Liberal Roots to a Green Future

Tim Cooper

Strategy

When in 1980, shortly after the formation of the West German Green Party, one of its leading members, Rudolf Bahro, concluded that 'There has never been so much unhappiness as there is today in the rich countries ... even in the most impoverished of times', he was echoing an observation made over the years by countless other critics of industrial society. Well over a century earlier, as the negative effects of the industrial revolution became increasingly apparent, the philosopher John Stuart Mill asserted boldly that he held a contrary view to those who considered 'the normal state of human beings is that of struggling to get on ... trampling, crushing, elbowing and treading on each other's heels.'

This underlying spirit of anti-industrialism has prevailed ever since nations began mass production, and has been particularly prominent in British society. The conflict between industrial and anti-industrial pressures in our society did not, however, play a major part in *political* debate until a growing awareness of the ecological threats became apparent in the early 1960s. Even today the main focus of political debate is around the relative merits of private and public means of providing goods and services, and green politics, which seeks to bring the industrialist/anti-industrialist debate centre-stage, has as yet had only a minor impact.

Signs of change are becoming increasingly apparent, and

most young people today are considerably more aware of global environmental problems and their political implications than previous generations. As the World Commission on Environment and Development pointed out in their 1987 report, *Our Common Future*: 'Most of today's decision makers will be dead before the planet suffers the full consequences of acid rain, global warming, ozone depletion, widespread desertification and species loss. Most of today's young voters will be alive.' The fact that the proportion of young people voting for the Greens in West Germany is three times greater than that of the middle aged and elderly reflects this increased awareness.

At the heart of any truly radical political agenda for the twenty-first century must be the planet. Humankind's most basic instinct is to survive, and the earth's life-support systems, upon which humankind depends for survival, are suffering irreversible damage. Make this connection – that we are dependent upon the earth's life-support systems and are threatened by the damage that they are suffering – and the raw nerve of our most primary instinct is touched. Politicise this connection, and the vital need is recognised for the new political agenda to be based on *ecology*, our understanding of how plants, animals, humans and institutions exist in relation to their environment. This is the starting point for green politics, the politicisation of ecology. Our fundamental premise is that solutions to the most critical problem facing humankind – the threat to our survival – cannot be found except through a greater appreciation of the interdependence of all creation. This must lead on to a practical response, which is the task before us.

Key Principles for the New Agenda

Ecology must lie at the heart of the philosophy underpinning the new political agenda. It should be a holistic philosophy, in recognition of the interconnectedness of different facets of society. One myth which needs exploding at the outset is that there are such things as 'green issues', normally identified as those pertaining to the natural environment, countryside policy in particular.

This is a serious misunderstanding of the very essence of green philosophy, as it implicitly presumes the existence of issues which *cannot* be embraced within such a philosophy. Human wellbeing is obviously influenced by other factors in addition to the condition of the natural environment. To understand the holistic nature of green philosophy demands an awareness that it is simply not credible to compartmentalise and thereby isolate particular issues, such as the environment.

To do so is to abuse the term 'green'. A cursory glance at the general election manifesto of the Green Party, for example, would confirm that the green philosophy embraces the entire spectrum of political issues, and regards them as wholly interconnected.

Having established that the political agenda for the next century must be rooted in ecology and holistic in its approach, if it is to achieve the kind of fundamental transformation in society which is necessary it should embrace four key principles.

First is the principle of *good stewardship*. There needs to be an unequivocal acceptance that sustained economic growth, as conventionally measured, is neither feasible nor desirable. The green philosopher E F Schumacher, in his classic book *Small is Beautiful*, wrote that 'modern man has built a system of production that ravishes nature and a type of society that mutilates man.' The aforementioned WCED report *Our Common Future* points out that industrial production had grown more than fifty-fold in the past century, and that seven times as many goods are produced today as in 1950. While some allowance must be made for the increased resource efficiency of modern production processes, it remains a disturbing fact that a typical growth rate of 3% implies consumption doubling every 24 years. Our finite planet can cope with basic need, but not with unrestrained greed.

An important corollary is that economic growth, far from improving human wellbeing, in many respects leads to a deterioration in the quality of life. One of the most important of modern British economists, E.J. Mishan, was vehemently critical in an essay entitled 'The Growth of Affluence and the Decline of Welfare' of the argument that economic expansion is a precondition to social progress and individual fulfilment. Fred Hirsch's 1977 book *Social Limits to Growth* further exposed the flaws in the assumption that growth necessarily makes society happier.

Our new agenda must take account both of the demands of a post-industrial economy and also of a post-materialist culture. In this it will echo the West German Green, Rudolf Bahro, in his call for 'unilateral industrial disarmament'. It will acknowledge that the necessary cultural transformation can only take place if there is full appreciation of people's non-material needs, and if people become motivated through a commitment from the heart which is essentially spiritual.

The second principle is *empowerment*. If people are to be liberated and fulfilled, they must first be empowered, and for this the prerequisites are social justice and political devolution.

Justice demands equality of opportunity, which in turn demands a radical redistribution of wealth; true justice cannot prevail in a society in which privilege can be purchased and passed on between generations. Access to resources, including land, financial capital and education and training facilities, is also essential and ought to be provided equitably to people of different backgrounds. Our new agenda must offer people the promise that they will be empowered to live as they choose so long as this does not impose on the freedom of others, and that they will genuinely become more self-reliant and free from constraints imposed either by the privilege of the few or by government.

Devolution of power to local communities will be a part of the process of empowerment. In recent years the reverse trend has been evident, with a Conservative administration concentrating power in central government. Despite their claim to advocate small scale enterprise, the Tories have done nothing to stem the trend towards a 'big is beautiful' society, in which power has become concentrated in ever larger industrial conglomerates, schools, hospitals, farms, building societies and other institutions.

A third principle is that of *participation*. The new agenda must challenge the sense of apathy felt by many people when faced with political and moral dilemmas. So often individuals excuse themselves from active involvement in politics and avoid making the difficult moral decisions this involves by resorting to the argument that as individuals they would make little impact on society as a whole. They disregard the words of Edmund Burke: 'The only thing necessary for the triumph of evil is for good men to do nothing.'

We need to inform the public that acquiescence to the present system is a form of conservatism. People are taking decisions which are essentially political when they choose their particular lifestyle. Whether it be switching their savings to one of the increasing number of ethical investment trusts, or refusing to eat meat or eggs where the animal has been reared in intensive conditions, these decisions ultimately affect not just the producers but also the priorities of political parties.

Our agenda must be founded upon participatory (as distinct from representative) democracy. It must at the very least include the introduction of a fair electoral system, such as the Additional Member System, and the abolition of the electoral deposits, which deter independent candidates and small parties from participation in the political system.

The fourth principle is *nonviolence*. Violence is not solely restricted to physical attacks: in a far deeper sense it is a cultural phenomenon in which society is shaped by the ultimate ability of dominant individuals or groups to get their way by force or mastery.

Thus in a very real sense we can speak of industrialists' violence against nature, by which the harmonious balance within the created order is destroyed through their ability to force change and thus destroy nature's balance.

Equally the implications of the *potential* physical dominance of a man over a woman, or a militaristic nation over a less aggressive nation, has implications for day-to-day relationships, irrespective of whether violence is actually used. Our new agenda must create forms of conflict resolution fit for mature people in the twenty-first century, rather than the caveman's club-over-the-head approach.

The Liberal and Green Traditions

In developing a strategy for transforming society according to this agenda, past political traditions offer useful insights. While the principles outlined above contain elements of libertarianism, anarchism, feminism, pacifism and socialism, my belief is that the tradition in which they are most clearly represented is radical liberalism and, further, that this tradition extends logically into the emerging analysis of the Greens.

The main bridges between liberal and green thinking were put in place in 1848, 1979 and 1988. In 1848 the liberal philosopher John Stuart Mill created a vision of an economy which took account of the limits to growth. 'The increase in wealth is not boundless,' he argued, 'the stationary state of capital and wealth . . . would be, on the whole, a very considerable improvement on our present condition.' He opposed the materialism of the politicians of his time: 'Those who do not accept the present very early stage of human improvement as its ultimate type may be excused for being comparatively indifferent to the kind of economical progress which excites the congratulations of ordinary politicians: the mere increase of production and accumulation.'

Human improvement would instead come about through 'all kinds of mental culture and moral and social progress'; broadly speaking, to use Mill's terms, the 'Art of Living' rather than the 'art of getting on'. Herman Daly and E.F. Schumacher, the two economists identified most closely with the green movement, both draw heavily upon such thinking.

In more recent times a growing awareness of the deepening ecological crises led the Liberal Party Assembly at Margate in 1979 to approve a motion which declared that 'sustained economic growth, as conventionally measured, is neither feasible nor desirable.' For a moment it seemed possible that the Liberals might recover a sense of urgency and vision and move towards adopting a radical green programme. But the Liberal leadership steered the party away from reviving the idea of a stationary state (or 'zero growth') economy, and such radicalism was destined for the dustbin when links began to be forged with the Social Democratic Party. The alliance with the SDP led critics such as Ian Bradley to point out that: 'The Liberals have become a party of too much organisation and too few ideas. Tactics tend to predominate over policies. This is out of keeping with their historic rôle as the seekers of new wisdom for a new age.'

The Liberal leadership throughout the 1980s appeared unable to portray a clear identity for liberalism. The party adopted a centrist approach, focusing attention on its 'moderation' compared to Conservative and Labour instead of developing and communicating to the public the implications of creating a society based on a liberal philosophy.

This led the political commentator Hugo Young to argue that David Steel 'has failed to produce any compelling vision of a Liberal or any other kind of non-Thatcherite Britain.' William Rees-Mogg went even further in suggesting that a genuine liberal is 'something David Steel has never been.' He continued: 'Certain elements of Liberal beliefs have been suppressed in the Steel years – they are much better argued by those like Simon Hughes or Tony Greaves, who genuinely believe in them. The Liberals with all their eccentricities are far from being a modern, technocratic social democratic party; they have a green heart.'

Certainly there are many people within the liberal tradition who sought to move the party in a genuinely radical direction. They were however deliberately marginalised by the Liberal leadership on every possible occasion.

Aware that many Liberals had over several years become increasingly disillusioned at the blandness and compromise created through the party's links with the SDP, I formed Green Voice in the autumn of 1987 as a network of Liberals and Greens who 'wanted the main alternative to Conservative and Labour to combine the best traditions of radical Liberalism with the emerging analysis of the Greens.'

At the first Green Voice public meeting in January 1988 Liberal MP Simon Hughes made it clear that his understanding of liberalism is essentially similar to green politics when he said: 'My politics is . . . about working with all creation, holistically,

respectfully, to do all that I can to ensure that every living crea-
ture has the best possible quality of life. My daily concern must
be to lead people away from the distraction of believing that,
apart from the basics of food, shelter, housing, clothing and
health, other materialistic possessions are *fundamentally*
important, or necessary to true happiness, self-discovery or
self-fulfilment.'

The centrality of ecology to Hughes's thinking is such that, in
an essay co-written with Nick Townsend, the most critical difference between the liberalism of the former Liberal Party and
the libertarianism of Mrs Thatcher is considered to be the different view each takes of the environment. In other words, green
politics forms the cutting edge which distinguishes liberalism
from Thatcherism. Thus in the important contemporary political debate concerning choice, the liberal democratic and green
response is similar: the use of the earth's resources must
involve restraint and sharing in order that choice is not cur-
tailed for future generations and for the people throughout the
world who live in poverty. The legacy of Thatcherism, in stark
contrast, is an understanding of choice which accepts the arbit-
rariness of the market and the survival of the fittest, or 'who
exploits, wins'.

Any fusion of radical liberalism and green politics will take
place in spite of the distinctly different starting points of the
two philosophies. The preamble to the former Liberal Party
constitution stated that its 'chief care is for the rights and
opportunities of the individual', while the starting point for the
Green Party is to acknowledge the vital importance of our
whole environment.

This distinction reflects the different eras in which the parties were founded. The Liberal Party emerged at a time when
the key issue of the day was the need to liberate the individual
from the power of the state and the church, to create a more
representative government and to allow for religious dissent.
The Green Party was formed in an era of ecological crisis, to
liberate the planet from the life-destroying forces of greed,
short-sightedness, carelessness and selfishness on the part of
humankind.

To accept that all life is interconnected is to accept the inextricable links between each individual and the environment, between 'person' and 'planet'. We can then take liberal democratic politics and green politics beyond their separate starting points and see how the philosophies interrelate. Liberalism without a green dimension threatens to offer individuals the freedom to destroy the planet and, in so doing, would deny the right of children and all future generations – and other species – to inherit and enjoy a healthy environment. Such a philosophy would promise the liberty of self-destruction. Green politics without a liberal dimension leads at best to a misguided framework for understanding the natural order – in which, for example, ants might be accorded equal rights with humans – and, at worst, to an implied eco-authoritarianism whereby the protection of the planet is put before the need to maintain civil liberties. Thus there is an essential bridge between liberalism and green politics. It is not just a question of optional complementarity. Divorced, the philosophical implications are positively disturbing.

Neither Right nor Left

One of the aims of our political strategy must be to convey to the public a greater depth of understanding of the nature of ideologies and their implications. Good presentation will be crucial. Our agenda will offer an alternative political direction which is visionary and *exciting*, in stark contrast to centrism, which is essentially 'splitting the difference' between the policies of the left and the right and consequently arriving at a set of bland proposals which inspire nobody.

Sara Parkin, in a speech at the Third Congress of the International Greens, described it thus: 'We are trying to shift the cleavage so it becomes a green/non-green one instead of a left/right one . . . we want to bend and then break up today's political continuum until it has greens at one end and the non-greens of both left and right suddenly finding themselves in the same political bed as the other.'

Jonathon Porritt uses the analogy of the motorway of industrialism, on which the travellers are using different vehicles and different lanes – left, right and centre – but all are heading in the same direction, towards an abyss. The greens reject the direction, not merely the choice of lane. Porritt argues that the similarities between the two dominant ideologies of the left and right are of greater significance than their differences: 'Both are dedicated to industrial growth . . . to a materialist ethic . . . and to unimpeded technological development. Both rely on increasing centralisation . . . both insist that the planet is there to be conquered, that big is self-evidently beautiful, and that what cannot be measured is of no importance.'

In developing this new political alternative, socialism is thus rejected alongside conservatism. Authentic green politics denies certain fundamental premises of socialism, in particular its class-based analysis and strategy. The most powerful critique of socialism as conventionally understood comes from Rudolf Bahro who, though describing himself as a socialist as well as a green, produces analysis which discards so much traditional socialism that the term seems no longer appropriate. Bahro argues that the historic mission of the proletariat is an illusion because Marx did not foresee that the contradiction between capitalist production and nature would become acute. The socialist goal of 'the general emancipation of humankind' is now impossible without overcoming the ecological crisis. Thus Bahro calls for a 'fundamental regrouping of forces' revolving around long-term human interest, putting 'life interests' before 'class interests' and involving a 'historic compromise . . . between all forces that seek the preservation and further development of . . . civilisation.'

Moreover, there needs to be 'a revaluation of values within the organised working class' to shift the centre of gravity of their concern away from a narrow 'institutionalised wage struggle'. The ecology crisis will result in the end of capitalism, however, it will not be through the 'working class' rising up against the capitalist system; rather it will be through the widespread adoption of a new order of values in response to ecological constraints, and a move away from materialism.

The Greens' theory of social change is considerably closer to that of Arnold Toynbee than that of Karl Marx. Marx argued that the prime moving forces of human history lay in the material sphere, and in particular the process of production. In contrast Toynbee viewed changing ideas and perceptions, stimulated by 'creative minorities', as critical. E.F. Schumacher wrote of the essential need for 'metaphysical reconstruction', while Jonathon Porritt has written: 'Some kind of spiritual commitment, or religion in its true meaning (namely, the reconnection between each of us and the source of all life), is a fundamental part of the transformation that ecologists are talking about . . . stripped of a spiritual dimension, politics in today's world is a hollow shell.'

We must tap the altruism, compassion and enlightened self-interest within individuals. The transformation of society through these means will be evolutionary in the sense of being gradual, but revolutionary in terms of the consequences.

Critical differences between socialism and green politics became highly visible at a seminar on 'green socialism' at the Socialist Conference held in Chesterfield in 1987. Participants fell into one of two camps, according to whether they considered the primary obstacle to liberty and fulfilment to be *capitalism* (a system which generates power for those who derive income from owning capital) or *industrialism* (a system in which devotion to industrial pursuits is accorded the highest status). While the main target for socialism is the transfer of *ownership* of the means of production to the 'working class', the target for greens is the transformation of the *values* of individuals, which we believe determine the nature of society and, specifically, the scale of industrial production within that society.

The sight of Eric Heffer at the Socialist Conference calling on 'professional people who wear smart ties . . . to understand that they too are part of the working class' was confirmation of the ideological disarray of socialism. Is the affluent, trendy Brixton-based yuppie, who sets up as a wholefood shopkeeper or printer, a member of the proletariat? Or the bricklayer who invests the £600 per week reported to be offered on London docklands building sites in the shares of privatised companies? These are today's realities which render socialism redundant.

The inherent materialism within socialist thinking casts further doubt on its validity. It presumes that the increased consumption of material goods and services, even beyond the basic necessities of life, brings greater human fulfilment, whilst at the very heart of the new agenda must be a rejection of such an assumption. People are not liberated through affluence and riches. To quote Mill: 'The best state for human nature is that in which, while no-one is poor, no-one desires to be richer, nor has any fear of being thrust back, by the efforts of others to push themselves forward.' Once people's basic necessities are provided for, a true sense of liberty is more likely to be gained by the abandonment and renunciation of material things than by their accumulation.

A further subtle distinction can be made. Conventional socialist analysis promises liberation for particular sectors of society perceived to be disadvantaged. Green politics, in contrast, aims to liberate all, *including the rich.* Socialism, being essentially materialist, sees no need to liberate rich people; its assumption is that their wealth has already made them fulfilled. A similar argument can be applied to sexual politics. While socialists tend to emphasise the liberation of women, greens wish equally to liberate *men.* The assumption of many socialists is that men's power and dominance makes them fulfilled, but the reality is very different, and many would prefer to undertake different roles if only social norms did not pressurise them towards the traditional stereotype.

A Realignment

My conclusion is that our strategy to implement the new agenda is thus rather different from a realignment of the *left,* and certainly involves more than a 'coalition of the dispossessed'. Those who wish to join together in the quest for a new politics based on the tradition of radical liberalism and the emerging analysis of the greens should reject the conventional thinking of both left and right alike.

Our realignment must from the outset be welcoming to all, even those from the 'right', who express a sincere interest in restoring fecundity to the earth and bringing liberty to all its inhabitants through democratic and non-violent means. Our agents for change will include the 'romantic conservatives' identified as environmentalists by Ralf Dahrendorf, as well as libertarian socialists of the utopian tradition. Women, who bear the children of the next generation – whose planetary inheritance we are seeking to protect – will have a special interest and role to play. The young, particularly students, will be particularly attracted by our long term vision and our idealism.

The electoral ineffectiveness of the green movement must end. The Green Party has only around 8,000 members. It is not enough. We need to inspire and draw together a much more substantial group of like-minded people. As the new agenda must be rooted in ecology, one priority must be to gain the support of the three million members of environmental groups in Britain. Greenpeace claims over 100,000 supporters, while Friends of the Earth has around 50,000. In addition CND has had a quarter of a million, and more conservative organisations such as the National Trust and the Royal Society for the Protection of Birds claim over one million and 400,000 members respectively. While not all environmentalists accept the radical implications of green politics, Philip Lowe and Jane Goyder are right to suggest in their book *Environmental Groups in Politics* that 'Perhaps the greatest failing of environmental groups in the 1970s has been their inability to translate their massive numerical support into an appreciable political force.' This realignment must be achieved 'from the bottom up'. Green Voice has indeed already begun to develop a network of supporters within different regions of the country; if it succeeds in expanding it will be through ordinary people in villages, towns and cities agreeing to co-operate together and attracting support for their campaigning activities.

A Green Deadline?

One of our tasks must be to unite people from different political backgrounds. Prior to the formation of the Social and Liberal Democratic Party, however, it became apparent that even those within the Liberal Party who felt an affinity with green thinking intended to join the new party until after the first or second of its assemblies; only once these were over would they consider leaving it. At the same time, despite a disappointing average vote of 1.4% in the 1987 General Election, there has been no inclination among Green Party activists to leave the party and seek to influence the direction of one of the larger parties.

One mechanism to consolidate Greens in one or other party might be for a target date to be set. Greens in the Social and Liberal Democratic party should create a **litmus test** for their party (those in the Labour Party could do the same). The test should be the acceptance by their party of four fundamental policy stances by the end of the decade:

1. *economic policy* must be framed around an understanding that sustained economic growth as conventionally measured is neither feasible nor desirable, and acceptance of the need for a substantial redistribution of wealth;
2. *defence policy* must be based on a non-nuclear strategy and unilateral steps must be taken by Britain as a contribution to global nuclear disarmament, including the imediate unconditional cancellation of Trident;
3. *energy policy* must focus on conservation, increased efficiency and the development of renewable sources, with all nuclear reactors to be shut down within four years;
4. *agriculture policy* must be based upon organic methods and a reduced use of chemical fertilisers and pesticides, and factory farming methods should quickly be phased out.

This list is necessarily highly selective, but incorporates essential priorities of the green movement. Were members of the SLD to be successful in gaining acceptance of these policies, and it proves to be a party with principles, there might be no need for a separate Green Party. The party is only a means to an end: the creation of a sustainable, just, decentralised, peaceful society. We cannot afford party chauvinism. If, however, the new party fails to develop an inspiring and visionary programme as outlines above (which currently appears more likely) in keeping with these policy stances, its green members will only retain their integrity if they leave and join the Green Party. A conference at the turn of the decade might facilitate this process. The autumn 1989 SLD Assembly could, with so much at stake, prove a *very* interesting event.

It may be argued that such policies as those set out above are too radical, and that to be electable a more conservative programme must be offered. I do not believe this to be so. No party based on pragmatism rather than principle is going to inspire and attract the large number of grass-roots activists needed if the parties of the left and the right are to be defeated.

The SLD and the Green Party are either going to converge or diverge. There are many within the SLD who sense an affinity with the Green Party, but who wish to remain in a party closer to the corridors of power. If there is convergence, might there not be scope for a greater degree of electoral co-operation between members of the parties? Nationwide pacts agreed by party leaders are unlikely (they would raise considerable difficulties, since the Greens are too non-hierarchical and decentralised to appoint national leaders!). However, local parties might consider informal agreements. These have already occurred in the past; in May 1986 Green councillors were elected in two local authorities after the Alliance decided not to field opposing candidates. A '1 for 3' trade-off might be considered in some local authorities where the Greens 'might' have sufficient resources to put up candidates in only some seats. Radical SLD candidates would, in return for not competing against them, get a 'clear run' in, say 3 out every 4 seats being contested. The likelihood of the Greens getting a foothold in local authorities and of the SLD winning control of councils would thereby be enhanced. However in order to achieve a society which is both liberal and green, we will also need to operate outside of the electoral arena.

The process of change must be nonviolent, but I believe that we must reject the argument of Fritjof Capra when he suggests that 'conflict should be minimzed in times of social transition.' The conservatism of British people, which borders of an unhealthy mix of indifference, fatalism and sheer apathy, is one of the crucial obstacles to the kind of social and political transformation that we are seeking. We must engage in the kind of tactical grass-roots civil disobedience which has been the hallmark of much radical protest, because it has proved a necessary prerequisite for a vast bulk of progressive change in society. This will inevitably result in conflict. We must extend the kind of displays of protest carried out by Greenpeace into new areas. Pedestrians who suffer fumes and noise from passing heavy lorries or aeroplanes, patients who are sent swiftly away with useless pills instead of true remedies for illness, shoppers who are offered food contaminated with pesticide residues – all should look for highly visible forms of protest to express their innermost passions against the present system. We should not shy away from publicly embarrassing those who inflict massive social and environmental costs upon the public, whilst reaping the economic benefits.

Another means of transforming society is to encourage millions of people to take part in an active boycott of all products which are unnecessary and environmentally destructive. One of the characteristics of modern Britain identified by Jeremy Seabrook in a 1987 *Green Line* article called 'The Green Movement and the Renewal of Social Hope' is a growing faith in the power of money. We can turn this to our advantage by treating seriously the possibility of transforming the production process through acting *en bloc* as green consumers. This has been very effective in, for example, making the food industry reduce the amound of additives it uses. The green movement could build upon this success by leafletting shoppers on other issues. A leaflet with photographs of factory farm conditions would prick the conscience of any civilised person.

This is not to propose support for 'green capitalism'. There is a very substantial difference between the conventional understanding of a green society and a capitalist system characterised by expansion of production, consumption and profit. They are far from being compatible; the methods and motives of capitalists, as typically understood, are utterly at odds with the restraint, moderation and non-aggressiveness of greens.

The kind of comprehensive green philosophy which will

enable the liberation of humankind and the whole planet from the forces of destruction is still in need of development. The task of clarifying the practical implications of our basic principles is urgent. Can the grave problem of overpopulation be tackled through liberal means? Can unilateralism perhaps be seen as a form of nationalism, blind to the fact that radioactive pollution does not respect national boundaries? Even more controversially, to what extent does green politics, by highlighting the rights of generations yet unborn, have implications for the abortion debate? Finding answers to such difficult questions as these might be helped by the creation of a series of think tanks and an independent newspaper or journal.

Our politics must be worked out in the light of the changes in the political climate during the 1980s. Former MP Michael Meadowcroft has condemned the failure of liberalism to capture the 'anti-collectivist' agenda in the late 1970s, arguing that it led to a Conservative Party which promoted *individualism*, self-advancement whatever the cost to others, rather than *individuality*, appreciation of and encouragement for diversity within humankind. In the eighteenth century Rousseau identified a similar distinction, between 'amour-propre', selfish interest, and 'amour de soi', enlightened self-interest. Individualism is rooted in selfishness, while enlightened self-interest is motivated by an urge to survive and to give and receive satisfaction.

The distinction between the two can and must be defined in terms of how the environment is perceived and used. Thus Simon Hughes and Nick Townsend conclude their 1987 *Radical Quarterly* essay: 'The political battles of the future will be between, on the one side, the politics of liberty, community and what might be called 'greenery', and, on the other, the politics of arbitrary, extreme inequality, sanctified by an elaborate ideological disguise labelled . . . economic choice.'

Our task is therefore to define fully the nature of the attack on liberty, community and ecology, and to provide an alternative. Anti-materialism has rarely been tapped effectively by politicians of the left and the right, whose constant appeal is to people's instincts of greed. We must, in contrast, address our appeal to their anti-materialist instincts, which are far more widely held than most politicans appreciate.

In all things we must be bold and courageous, innovative and fun-seeking. Only then will we succeed.

Moves Towards a Green Future

Jean Lambert

The major problem facing us in the late twentieth century is unlike any we have known before. The very support systems upon which we all depend for our survival – clean air, clean water, fertile soil, stable climate – are all under threat. We can no longer look at the oceans and believe they can go on for ever when we think of the chemical and radioactive waste we dump in them, the tons of sewage and industrial waste we expect them to cleanse, or the acid rain that continues to fall into them. Similarly, the earth is suffering the effects of vast chemical over-use and persistent cash-cropping, sucking the soil dry of its nutrients and leaving it open to erosion and desertification.

The environmental problems resulting from the industrial world's attitude to the planet, that it is something to be exploited in order to give up as much of its riches as fast as possible and make us wealthier, are massive. Humankind's real wealth lies in the health of the planet – if it dies, so do we all: our environment and our social well-being are inextricably interlinked.

The challenge for us all is to find ways of changing our expectations, our values and our politics to cope with this new and horrific development in additon to the evils of poverty, both in Britain and worldwide, continuing conflicts over religion and resources, and the death-dealing arms race.

The Growth of the Greens

The only political movement which is really trying to come to terms with all these problems is the Greens. Since the early 1970s, this new political movement has been growing and, while policies differ from country to country, the underlying principles of each party and their long-term visions are shared. Their perception of politics and the future is:

Holistic – recognising the links between different areas;

Planet-based – understanding the basic importance of the planet's health and seeing ourselves as part of a life continuum;

Sustainable – realising that there are limits to growth and that we must develop patterns of living that can be maintained, whether in agriculture, economics or social structures;

Socially Just – our futures are inter-linked: there can be no real peace or sustainability if people are deprived or oppressed;

Democratic and Participative – we have the right to decide our future; only by co-operation and understanding can we develop sustainable societies, not through the continuation of power-controlling hierarchies;

Decentralised – the smaller-scale is more open to democratic control and less vulnerable to external forces.

Unlike conventional politics, which places economic criteria centre-stage, the Greens have a wider base of values, recognising the importance of the spiritual and creative aspects of individuals, and the need for a balance between 'feminine' values such as compassion, co-operation and humility and the 'masculine' ones such as assertiveness and decisiveness, so valued in our present political system.

This seems a distant vision – a future of peace and justice in a green and clean world. What are the chances of even moving towards that vision in the UK by the year 2000?

The Present State of UK Politics

Mrs Thatcher's statement at the start of the 1987 general election campaign about 'setting the political agenda until the end of the century' seems to have thrown the conventional opposition into a state of disarray. The current political scene is not one in which different visions of the future vie for the public's approval, but which appears instead as one where the opposition competes with the government, not about basic differences but about amounts spent, whether it be on education, housing, the NHS or social security. The Labour Party is increasingly being fashioned in the image of the Conservatives.

'Labour Listens' is a fudged admission that the official opposition no longer has a clear view of what its political purpose is, nor of how to achieve the goals it can agree on. The 'battle' for the leadership between Kinnock and Benn is already being used to prepare the public and party for Labour's failure in the next general election by being presented as a dangerous 'diversion' from the fight against Thatcherism, rather than *for* socialism. It is surely difficult to divert anything that doesn't really know in which direction it is travelling!

What is really happening within the Labour Party, and within other parties of the left such as the Communists, is that they are having to cope with the growing realisation that their political philosophy and analysis may have been correct for the nineteenth century – a time of industrial expansion and colonialism set alongside abject poverty – but which prove grossly inadequate when viewed in a context of industrial decline, environmental degradation, the demands of the non-industrialised world for its rightful share of the world's wealth, and the rise of feminism. Given its historical background as an industrial, male-dominated movement based mainly on material measures of well-being, it is not surprising that the socialist left cannot provide the vision and direction that is needed *now*.

The challenge of the 'mould-breaking' third force in British politics has now receded. What in 1981 held the promise of a democratic, decentralised, environment-friendly form of politics based on dynamic co-operation, has rapidly declined. Instead of being a partnership of equals, offering the electorate a chance to break the predictable see-saw of two-party politics and then progress to something more open, the SDP and Liberals made the fatal mistake of trying to create a third party out of two. Rather than exploit the possibility of *challenging* the existing system, the Alliance tried to become part of it. It was this compromise that, I believe, led to the loss of Alliance seats and the dissatisfaction within the two parties. The supposed public 'confusion' about the two leaders has been used as a superficial shorthand to gloss over the real problem – the lack of clarity and vision about what the two parties wanted to achieve in terms of change.

What of the Conservatives, this seemingly invincible force that the opposition is struggling to stop? Let us look more closely at their 'strength'. At local level there are more opposition councillors than there are Tories. Many Conservative local councillors are deeply unhappy about changes being made by the Tory government: for example, the fact that local councils will only be able to raise 25% of their own revenue as a result of the 1988 Local Government Bill, or the problems resulting in their educational provision because of progressive orders to cut spending. The Conservatives have almost total control within Parliament due to their majority of MPs, but how secure and sustainable are they? It is privatisation and North Sea oil revenues that have supported tax cuts: these are both non-sustainable, finite sources of finance.

There is disagreement within the parliamentary party over such issues as local government finance, the role of the welfare state, defence procurement and the privatisation of basic utilities such as electricity and water. The Conservatives have shown themselves vulnerable to internal and external pressure on such issues as student grants, nurses' pay, levels of housing benefit and proposed NIREX test sites.

The government will respond to pressure if applied in the correct places. Fundamentally, however, the whole direction of Conservative policy is unsustainable and extremely vulnerable, relying as it does on increasing our share of European and world trade when we still rely heavily on imports for many basics (food included), which makes us the easy victims of fluctuations in currency values and international markets. For a party that likes to present itself as protector of Britain's independence, it is ironically moving us even further towards economic, military and political dependence on others.

It has, however, already set its own scapegoat in place. By encouraging the portrayal of Margaret Thatcher as the all-powerful, domineering 'iron lady', Conservative Ministers,

MPs and party members have neatly abdicated their own responsibility for what is done in the government's name, thus allowing them to dump their leader and change direction when the situation demands – and it will!

At present the nationalist parties (Plaid Cymru and the SNP) seem to be offering a more attractive agenda than the 'big three', but unless they can build the concept of sustainability into their programmes they will remain no more than political shadows. Nationalism based on industrial growth and ideas of conventional full employment will not see us into the twenty-first century.

The Challenge for the Greens

The conventional political scene thus presents us with a vacuum in terms of political direction and purpose which the Greens should be able to fill with their own vision and practical alternatives. How easy will this be?

In terms of straight electoral success under our present grossly-unjust 'first-past-the-post' system, the election of Green Party parliamentarians and majority local councils could be a long and expensive haul. There is also diffidence amongst some Greens about standing for office in this way – by participating in what is seen as a corrupt and unrepresentative system they feel that the Green presence validates it, and that we should therefore shun elections and create an alternative society instead. There are also those who feel that it is far more important for individuals to change their own consciousness before trying to change society. Others still feel that there are key single issues, such as campaigning against nuclear weapons, which must be addressed first in order to reduce immediate dangers.

Were Greens to believe that there is only one right way to progress, we would be in danger of spending so long squabbling amongst ourselves that the world would die around us. As it is, most Greens can see the pressing need for change in all aspects of our lives, both personal and political, and recognise that only by working in a variety of constructive, nonviolent ways can we begin the process of change. Since its foundation in 1973 as 'People', what is now the Green Party has seen a gradual shift in people's perceptions of the importance of green politics. Once dismissed as 'a single-issue party', it now sees politicians claiming that their own parties are 'green' – meaning they have environmental policies – and some have even come to see that 'green' is an overall form of politics rather than a collection of issues that can be incorporated into an already-existing manifesto.

At first the Green Party's response to other parties improving their environmental policies and thus claiming to be 'green' was scathing – pointing out the inherent inconsistencies of claiming to save the environment while continuing industrial policies that threatened it. The Party's more recent responses have still been sceptical but a little more welcoming – rather as one might encourage a child's first faltering footsteps in the hope that it will eventually understand what it is doing and walk confidently without support.

Also over the past few years we have seen a growing number of people declare themselves as green, thus showing the movement's growing appeal and making it more difficult for our opponents to write us off as irrelevant and transient. One cannot portray as 'ageing hippies' people as diverse as the Bishop of Durham, Ruth Rendell, Spike Milligan, Joanna Lumley, Boy George and Simon Hughes, MP – who have all described themselves as green or Green Party supporters. Electoral, academic and union support for the Greens is growing, as is interest from people of all ages and backgrounds.

People now recognise some of the problems, so the green movement's first phase of development – planting the awareness of our situation – is making progress. What Greens now have to develop are the ways to cope with increased awareness, and to use this awareness to bring about constructive and lasting change as rapidly as possible. Who knows how long we have before further Chernobyls or Sevesos occur, or before we irrevocably contaminate our water and air?

Towards a Strategy for Change

It is vitally important that any strategy for change within the UK is not one which is developed by the few to be imposed upon the many. Any lasting change must be built on foundations of co-operation and mutual trust – things that come particularly hard to politicians!

Those of us committed to working for a green future must realise that few people come to the green movement as 'perfect' Greens – understanding all the links and subtleties of a new form of politics: no one has this complete understanding. There are two main conclusions to be drawn from this: firstly, those who feel they understand more must make it easy for people to take small and positive steps and, secondly, we need to develop our philosophy, policy and activities. Green must be both practical and intellectual.

The 'small steps' may be those of changing one's lifestyle in terms of the resources we use and the things we buy: using public transport, a bike or our feet rather than a private car, or buying environmentally-sound washing-up liquid. Individuals can change their ways of handling relationships, trying to avoid dominating or being passive. They can change the way they vote – deciding to vote for people who ideas best express their own rather than the candidate most likely to win!

Such small changes are not of themselves likely to transform the world, but they do begin to set a climate in which further change is possible. The path of consumer choice may seem peripheral to some, in that it seeks to persuade large transnational producers to change their products rather than tackling the power structure they represent but, given that such companies are going to exist for the foreseeable future, they ought at least to be encouraged to produce less polluting, longer lasting, more resource-efficient products.

It is also important that individuals are provided with positive ways in which they can feel they are doing *something*. One of the most vital elements in creating a green future is providing a sense of empowerment to counter the present feelings of powerlessness and apathy. People should feel good about change.

Greens are too often accused of providing only 'gloom and doom' scenarios – leaving people with a sense of impending disaster and global problems that are too massive to comprehend, let alone prevent. It is essential that Greens examine the constituent parts of each problem and develop strategies for constructive change on a small scale, so that change becomes possible and people feel they can participate in it. The security and confidence needed to do something different is often underestimated by Greens. The green vision involves massive change and this will obviously be threatening to many individuals – this is the 'Greens want you sitting in the dark, shivering around a candle' scenario that the Central Electricity Generating Board or British Nuclear Fuels present of us.

Greens know that doing away with electricity produced from nuclear power plants won't have that effect, especially if we invest in energy conservation, but many people don't know that. Greens, therefore, have a responsibility to demonstrate that people can still be fundamentally safe, even if major changes are taking place. If anything is unsafe, it's a future based on unsustainable economics, food production and the nuclear industry!

A Green strategy for change must thus incorporate principles of empowerment, participation and positive reassurance.

Damage Limitation

Apart from individuals taking steps to change their own lifestyles and feeling they are contributing to a green future, what else is needed?

In the short term, there is an obvious need to limit the damage being caused to our planet and its people in order to prevent things getting worse. Here, I believe Greens have to be more selective and more organised in their opposition in order to achieve more than they have done in the past.

What should be the criteria for the selection of issues? I believe we should be active in two main directions: firstly, we should oppose those measures which remove democratic choice from people and, secondly, we should campaign against major environmental threats to our planet. The health of our democracy matters. If we want citizens to take responsibility for their own actions and the condition of the planet and its peoples, they must have the freedom to do that. In the UK the role of local government to determine its own social and economic priorities has been under attack for a numnber of years. Money for new-build housing and extensive renovation programmes has been cut back since the mid-70s; rate-capping has destroyed the ability of councils to raise revenue through the rates to provide for social needs.

The taking of economic power by central government has been accelerating. It is not, therefore, surprising that Greens have been vocal in their opposition to the Community Charge, but I believe they have ignored many of the surrounding issues. To attack the Community Charge because it takes no account of the ability to pay is fair criticism – it is a view shared by socialists, Greens, Liberals and some Tories. What Greens have failed to spell out is that the whole Local Government Finance Bill is a centralising Bill, designed to reduce still further the economic power of local government, and it is this which makes it particularly dangerous to the development of a green, decentralised society.

Green opposition to the Education Reform Bill has been negligible – yet here is legislation which among other things centralises the curriculum, determines school size, and lays down totally inadequate voting rules for the removal of community assets from the community on the say-so of a few. Where have the Greens been in their opposition to the possible removal of Development Studies from the curriculum or to the Secretary of State having the power to appoint Governors?

It is essential that Greens oppose centralising measures and work for the right to local, democratic control if there is to be any hope of a strong local level: the local level which is the basis of power in a green society. We need to examine new legislation in that light as a criterion for hard opposition: does it significantly shift power to the centre? If so, we should oppose it.

Protection of the environment is vital to Greens – without a healthy, safe environment, other things become irrelevant. A superb education system, adequate wealth for all, a great national health system are of no benefit if our air is poisoned, our water polluted and our soil barren. So what issues should we tackle in order to limit the damage to our environment?

In the West, we must continue our relentless opposition to nuclear power and weaponry, the environmental time-bomb that threatens the ecocide (total environmental destruction) of our planet. This one we can win. The possibility of the privatisation of electricity production has shown up the appalling economic state of nuclear power production: the new fast-breeder and fusion programmes are nowhere near commercial viability, and 'diversity of supply' can be assured in other ways. The Hinckley C enquiry and 'Stop Sizewell B' nonviolent, direct-action programme deserve all the energy and support that Greens can muster.

The 1989 European elections will provide an excellent platform for green opposition to the non-sustainable, environmentally-disastrous Common Agricultural Policy with its emphasis on quantity rather than quality, chemical input and factory farming.

Both our agricultural policy and our nuclear policy have grave implications for the developing world, and this dimension of global concerns is essential to green politics. For Greens, the world-view does not consist of single, competing nation-states, but of inter-linked communities. Environmental campaigning is not simply about local protection; it is about global survival. Thus our 'damage-limitation' campaigning should be based on what will protect and enhance individual and local democracy and the global environment.

Proposition Politics

I mentioned earlier the need for positive reassurance. Important though damage limitation is, by itself it will not bring about radical change; it will largely preserve the status quo. It is therefore necessary for Greens not to just be involved in 'opposition' politics, but also in 'proposition' politics – putting forward positive ideas, taking positive action and presenting a positive vision of the future. It is sometimes easy to become so involved in reacting to other people's proposals that we begin to argue in their terms, forgetting our own perspective and our own creativity.

Greens frequently talk in terms of acting locally, thinking globally, and it is at the local level that practical demonstrations of proposition politics can be very successful. Examples include local energy conservation projects, renewable energy projects, wholefood co-operatives, co-operative nurseries, small parks, community education, recycling and repair schemes, and so on. Such things are useful because they show the unaware, the worried or the sceptical that small-scale operations can be practical and manageable.

On a national level, we must be able to offer constructive proposals on a variety of areas, but I would see democracy and environmental improvement as priorities.

The introduction of proportional representation would clearly be of great value in opening up the democratic process, enabling a greater number of political viewpoints to be represented. It would not necessarily be a panacea for Greens – people have to be convinced by your arguments and your abilities before they will vote for you, but a more just form of representation is essential to opening up the political system. With such a reform in operation, the Trident weapons system would have been cancelled by now, there would be greater spending on social areas, and better transport and environmental policies – the nuclear expansion programme would have been halted!

Another step towards greater democracy, and probably environmental protection too, would be a Freedom of Information Act allowing us to have better information concerning such things as the testing of herbicides, and the real figures upon which the nuclear industry bases its cost projections.

In terms of environmental protection and resource conservation, Greens could propose a real energy conservation programme which would help poor and elderly people afford the heat they need; cut down on our use of finite fuels; reduce our sulphur contribution to acid rain; and obviate the need for nuclear power production.

Greens could also put forward powerful proposals to improve the quality of our food production, benefiting all consumers and the land at the same time, by promoting organic argiculture, diversification of products and varieties of foods. Better quality food would improve both our health and our environment.

Who Will Carry Out The Strategy?

The Green Party has about 8,000 members; there are Greens in all the other political parties struggling to change those institutions and their policies; the environmental pressure groups have an estimated membership of around three million (presumably with considerable overlap) and there are many more people who would consider themselves greens but who aren't members of anything. This makes up a large minority of the UK population, but if one is looking for practical examples of what has been achieved by this sizeable group, the answer is 'very little'.

What have been changing, however, are the perceptions that people have of what is important. Opinion polls show that people's concern for the environment is growing; that they are more aware of the economic issues underlying many of the developing world's environmental and agricultural problems, and so on.

This change of perception has come about partly through the actions and propaganda of green groups, but also through the work of the media, whose documentaries have shown the problems clearly, even though they may be wary of radical political solutions.

We should not assume, however, that those in the peace and environmental pressure groups necessarily have an understanding of the relationships between issues. There are Oxfam shop volunteers who objected to people leafletting outside the shops with 'Hungry for Change' leaflets (Oxfam's own campaign) because the material was 'political': it sought to demonstrate that people starve because of debt and environmental degradation, and that we need to examine the West's relationship with the developing world. Those who oppose NIREX prospecting for dumping sites in their own village may not be opposed to nuclear power. You can care deeply about a specific environmental issue, but until you see the links and realise that most things must change, you aren't a Green!

Pressure groups have to get their act together to construct a green future. There is a need for closer collaboration and strategic action from them as a group. With greater co-ordination, they would be a very powerful force for change. They have the authority of acknowledged expertise in many areas; they command enormous public support and sympathy. If the peace and environmental pressure groups really want the sort of changes they talk about, they need to be braver and clearer about where they want to go – presumably they want a situation where they no longer have to exist! Part of their problem, however, is their internal politics – only party allegiances can easily prevent real commitment to the politics of the future.

A key part of putting any green strategy into practice must be the education of those who have begun to realise there are problems, which will in turn assist the development of practical solutions. To this end we must use the sympathy that already exists within the broadcasting media and some sections of the press to put across green analysis and solutions. We must separate our feelings of suspicion and distaste about those who own the press and its lack of democracy from our ability to work with those people within the media who respect the Greens and believe we are correct in our views. If Greens ignore the media or refuse to co-operate with it, we really will be allowing 'them' to present us as they wish. To co-operate is not to sell out; to co-operate is to *work together* to achieve something.

We must also use the growing interest of students and academics to provide necessary research into alternative ways of living. Increasingly, engineering and science students do not wish to work for the military or big businesses. Greens have a responsibility to provide them with projects that are practical, positive and exciting.

For those who see politics as irrelevant or suspect – the vast majority of the population – Greens need to demonstrate that alternative politics does not mean yet more confrontational slanging matches, but that it can be co-operative, constructive and fun, and that it is an area where everyone can feel confident and valued. It is no accident that many women feel happy to represent the green perspective: it is a political philosophy in which everyone has value. We must not lose sight of this.

But how do we involve people; how do we prove that politics can be co-operative? I have already indicated certain issues and principles upon which Greens should campaign, but campaigning on our own is not always useful. It is right to work with pressure groups and other political parties on issues which are important: there are many things more vital than party chauvinism. The green cause needs to involve the politically active, the pressure group activist, the general public, and especially the disaffected – the poor, the unemployed, and those who suffer from racial discrimination.

Greens need all these people. We need to learn how to hear the message coming from many of the churches and other religious groups; from trade union members who can see what their jobs are doing to our planet; from people in our own communities who want to *do* something to change the world. This is the Greens' most important task – to make the links between the issues and the people.

And The Green Party?

Not surprisingly, I see the need for the continuation of the Green Party for the next five to ten years at least. I believe Greens need a political rallying point; imperfect though the party may be in its organisation and policies, it does have a sense of vision and purpose.

Greens in other parties need it as a reference point for their own policy development, and as a conscience. It may well be that such people will wish to leave their own parties and help to build something better. If the SLD doesn't develop really green policy and philosophy, if 'Labour listens' only to the voice of the political past, if the Conservatives continue to ignore those who care for the land rather than the property developer – then we shall see even more people joining the Green Party.

A second key period will be after the next general election, especially if the Conservatives are returned again and the traditional opposition is left further demoralised. The Green vision will then seem very attractive. The third period will be around the 1994 European elections which all Greens of whatever party *must* ensure take place under a PR system; we shall then see UK Greens joining their counterparts from the European mainland in the European Parliament. That, combined with the increasing number of Green Party councillors, will really spell political breakthrough – let us hope that it will not be too late.

By 2000

What might we then hope to see by the year 2000?
– a change in the political agenda where green politics is developing as *the* new politics;
– an end to the UK nuclear power programme and the reduction of nuclear weapons;
– change in agriculture towards 'environment-friendly' policies;
– tightened environmental protection;
– a massive energy conservation programme;
– the opening up of democracy;
– slowing of international trade;
– serious tackling of Third World debt.

It sounds a major task, but the signs are already there that it is not impossible. It is time for Greens to really take ourselves seriously and to believe that we can win. Let's face it – if Prince Philip believes that without action the future looks really bleak for his descendants, what hope is there for the rest of us!

We must learn to work together, to trust each other and ourselves. Together, we can change the future.

A Strategy For New Alliances

Peter Hain

Advocacy of 'alliances' or 're-alignments' is instinctively attractive to those of us who, by temperament and political experience, react against the sectarianism which disfigures almost every party or group.

Since it first surfaced in the 1960s, however, such advocacy has invariably been cloaked in a great deal of romanticism. The record is hardly encouraging. Aside from certain single issue campaigns – notable Stop the Seventy Tour, the Anti-Nazi League and CND – alliances at national level have been hard to forge. In the case of those exceptions, there was unofficial co-operation between elements within parties rather than open, official agreements.

Moreover, when leading figures, notably Jo Grimond, talked of a 're-alignment of the left', they defined 'left' in such a way as to exclude most who felt happy with the label. Sometimes the phrase was a euphemism for Lib-Labbery. Mostly it was describing a re-grouping of the centre.

It would be as well to put our cards on the table before discussion is opened up afresh. My starting point is that, for the foreseeable future, the Labour Party will remain the principal focus for the left and wider progressive forces. There are a number of reasons for this.

Labour's Pivotal Role

First, although Labour's political base has contracted, under the current electoral system the Party's parliamentary representation cannot be reduced to much under two hundred without demographic and political changes so fundamental as to be unpredictable. On the contrary, there is good reason to suppose that Labour will continue to recover from the depths of 1983, the outstanding question being at what rate.

Second, the electoral system will not change at least until a defeat of the Tories creates entirely new circumstances. And, as a matter of political fact, only Labour can beat the Tories under the existing system. Labour will therefore continue to be the major opposition to the Tories, though it remains to be seen whether the party can win sufficient popular support to win outright, or whether it will have to be content with becoming the largest party.

Third, the sad demise of radical liberalism means that the left's voice will be faint if not silent within the Liberal and Social Democrats. Having been a Young Liberal national officer until it became clear that the senior party could not be converted to our 'libertarian socialist' ideas, I joined Labour in 1977, warning that liberal radicalism was ebbing away as the party slid rightwards. Most YLs stayed to fight on, making some advances but gradually becoming respectable – pale shadows of the vibrant group which made such an impact in the late 1960s and early 1970s.

After the formation of the Alliance with the SDP in 1981, the radicals were repeatedly isolated and sidelined by the two party leaderships. That was the logical political result of the rightward momentum which gathered pace in the Liberal Party from the mid-1970s. Once the Liberals had firmly rejected the strategy of providing a radical alternative to Labour, there was only one option: to become soft Thatcherites.

The climax was the merger, the abortive Thatcherite statement by David Steel and Robert Maclennan confirming how deeply the rot had set in, with David Owen hovering like Banquo's Ghost over every policy discussion of the new party. The existence of the continuing SDP will act as a further blocking force against radicalism, because the SLD will cock a constant eye towards the Owenites in order to avoid being outflanked.

The fourth reason why Labour is likely to remain dominant on the left is that the other alternatives are too weak. Single issue politics has been in decline in recent years. Although individual pressure groups and campaigns will continue to play an important role, there is no prospect of aggregating them into a coherent political movement which could provide an alternative to the major parties. Elsewhere, the Communist Party is unlikely to grow out of its present, and much reduced, role as an interesting pressure group. The Socialist Workers Party could well become the major force on the organised left outside Labour's ranks but it will remain small, and its Trotskyist politics will exclude it from the broad democratic left movement.

The Greens are in a different position. Support for green politics is likely to grow, and the party could become influential if it constructs its strategy carefully. However, the Greens are also trapped by the electoral system. Like the rump of radical Liberals and all the autonomous movements, the Greens will be politically marginal without proportional representation: occasionally recognised for good ideas or energetic activity, but totally remote from exercising real power.

Fifth, Labour is in a better position than it has been for some time to lay claim to being the true voice of the left. Although there is a continuing debate within the party about its direction, Labour has restored its credibility. It has modernised and become much more progressive. Many local Labour parties have adopted a campaigning approach which overlaps with the best of 'community politics'. The old guard tammany hall politics and town hall fixing have largely been eclipsed by more open, democratic and participatory Labour parties and councils. In response to the growing strength of feminism, the party has made women's rights an important part of its practice and programme. Its support for non-nuclear defence and energy policies, coupled with a far-reaching programme to protect the environment, has given a strong green tint to the red flag. Labour's rejection of old-style nationalisation and its commitment to social ownership and industrial democracy has much in common with the decentralist, co-operative thrust of many radical forces outside the party. Its new commitment to decentralisation and devolution add to the gradual transformation – still to be completed – of Labour from a 'state socialist' to a more 'libertarian socialist' party.

The trade unions have also become more progressive and democratic. In recent years, unions have undergone changes more far-reaching than for generations. Opportunities for membership participation have been enlarged, the movement has been modernising itself, and there is an important, though not yet dominant, force moving towards a more campaigning, outward type of unionism which can engage politically with the wider community, rather than operating in the traditional pattern of narrow sectionalism.

Despite these changes, much still needs to be done to improve the labour movement. The argument here is not that Labour is ideal – far from it – but that any talk of re-alignment cannot by-pass the labour movement.

Extra-Parliamentary Politics

However, although Labour may be able to defeat the Tories *electorally*, it is unlikely to defeat Thatcherism *ideologically* without building wider alliances for change. Winning *elections* is vital – as is the process of modernising the Labour Party and projecting a vision of democratic socialism that is capable of attracting popular support again. But winning *power* cannot be done through a narrow parliamentary party perspective alone.

Power in Britain resides only fitfully and partially in parliament. It is concentrated outside, in the business community, the financial institutions, the foreign exchange markets, the civil service and the military élites. These extra-parliamentary – and frequently extra-democratic – forces cannot be challenged by playing the parliamentary game.

A successful strategy for socialist transformation will require a combination of winning parliamentary office and mobilising extra-parliamentary power through alliances for change that straddle parties and involve people in their own communities, workplaces or interest groups.

There is a further reason why Labour cannot hope to succeed fully by going it alone. Even in a post-Thatcherite Britain, the ideology of Thatcherism will retain a formidable residual influence. Since 1979 British society has been restructured in a fundamental way, and to change course in a leftward direction will require a depth and breadth of support which no single party can hope to encompass. It should be noted that the last major shift to the left in Britain – culminating in Labour's 1945 landslide – occurred because of a shift in the balance of class forces and the development of a popular consensus for change which the Attlee government came to express. Labour could not have carried through such a radical programme without mass support. Nor could it have succeeded unless the radical changes it instituted had been running with the grain of society's development. It is inconceivable that Labour could come into office in the 1990's and immediately carry through a radical programme unless a similar, broad consensus for change had been mobilised.

Having noted the background imperatives for re-alignment, what are the prospects for securing it? Out of the fiasco of the Liberal-SDP merger, there could be the opening for new alliances on the left, involving radical Liberals, the Greens, independents from single-issue groups and Labour's libertarian socialist strand. Whether this takes the form of actually joining the Labour Party should not necessarily be the main issue (though those parts of the radical liberal tradition unwilling to dissolve their politics into the merged party would be welcomed by Labour just as I was in 1977).

Far more important would be to establish a common network in which people could work together on specific projects. If the Thatcherite tide is to be reversed, it will require the left defined in its broadest sense to seek common ground and build alliances for change that are rooted outside parliament and the town hall. Recent examples have included the campaign against the anti-abortion Alton Bill and the fight for a decent national health service, but there needs to be discussion of a common political programme if the process is to go beyond individual campaigns.

Libertarian Socialism

What might such a programme include?

It would be rooted in the ideology of 'libertarian socialism', historically a minority strand in the socialist tradition, but one whose importance and validity has grown as the limits and authoritarianism of state socialism have been recognised. Libertarian socialists are not willing to subordinate democracy to the party or to hand over their autonomy and rights to some superior vanguard. Socialism is either inseparable from individual freedom and democratic rights or it is not worth having. Indeed, democracy and liberty are its starting points, not optional extras to be made available once the class war has been won. This implies a strategy for socialist transformation based upon empowering people, building for change from the bottom upwards rather than attempting to drop a new order into position from above.

There are many outside the Labour Party who could readily identify with such a political approach, even if they do not call themselves 'socialists'. Some will be sceptical about the extent of Labour's support for such a politics, and understandably so. However, the argument is not that Labour has suddenly been transformed into a pure libertarian socialist party. The point is that the party has been moving in that direction, and that the libertarian socialist currents within it provide the axis around which wider alliances can be built.

Fundamental to this approach is what has been termed 'third road politics'. Those currents on Labour's left who have been articulating third road politics reject both insurrectionism and reformism and advocate a strategy which combines the use of parliamentary change with extra-parliamentary struggle and campaigning. It thus stands apart both from Leninism which has so disfigured socialist politics, and the practice of past Labour governments which has so discredited it.

A Common Programme?

To draw up a common programme covering too ambitious a range of policies would render a wider network of alliances still-born. Nevertheless, there are some benchmarks.

A broad-based movement must defend basic civil rights and democratic principles against the frightening authoritarianism which is now the dominant characteristic of Thatcherite Britain. The list grows ever longer: suppressing *Spycatcher*; banning BBC programmes; making criminals out of investigative journalists who refuse to reveal their sources; attacking the rights of homosexuals and artistic expression through the insidious clause of the 1988 Local Government Act; concentrating power remorselessly into Whitehall as local government becomes an empty shell. Scotland's desire for devolution is arrogantly ignored, education becomes the property of the Secretary of State, and local health authorities are rendered impotent. All this would be common ground for radicals in the Labour Party, the ex-Liberals, the Greens and others.

There would also be broad agreement on a decentralist thrust, both to reverse Thatcherite centralism and to empower individuals – policies such as devolution for Scotland, an elected assembly for Wales, regional government for England, decentralisation of power to local government and down to neighbourhood councils and community resource centres. All of these would command wide support.

Electoral reform could be an obstacle, though not an insurmountable one if the case is not obsessively tied to either List systems or STV multi-member systems of proportional representation – for a critique see my 1986 book, *Proportional Misrepresentation*. An option which retains the accountability best expressed in single member constituencies, such as the Alternative Vote, would get a much more sympathetic hearing. Nobody can seriously deny that the existing system is unfair, but the principal PR alternatives are equally flawed. There needs to be a more open forum for dialogue and debate about electoral reform – always remembering that it cannot be part of a strategy for defeating Thatcherism since it cannot be delivered until that defeat has been accomplished. In other words, it would be wrong to make a fetish of PR, when there is so much else, maybe even including electoral reform, upon which agreement could be forged.

Policies such as a Freedom of Information Act and democratic control of the police and the security services would doubtless be agreed on the nod.

The principle of industrial democracy would also be widely accepted, even if clarification is needed on the precise form this might take. Care should be taken, however, to establish common ground on economic policy. Individual policies supported by Labour's left such as a statutory minimum wage or co-operatives could well have a wide appeal. But the question of extending social ownership and democratic control of the economy, so crucial to socialists, may be problematic for other radicals. Indeed there is a deafening silence amongst radical Liberals, Greens and other progressive groups outside the labour movement on key questions about the power of capital and policies to promote investment and full employment.

Greening British Politics

An important part of a new radical consensus would be the greening of Britain. The obvious linchpins would be a non-nuclear defence policy and a non-nuclear energy policy, and there is also common ground on a whole series of policies to protect the environment. A stumbling block could be the question of growth, though not necessarily if we are willing to discuss this rigorously, rather than resorting to sloganeering. There is no dispute on the left that rampant materialism, a ravenous appetite for non-renewable resources and an appalling catalogue of ecological destitution, has challenged the whole notion of economic growth in modern industrial society.

But the fact is that both the Third World and under-developed parts of industrial society desperately need economic growth. To deny that is to share complicity with the forces which have bred mass poverty and exploitation. Additionally, the existence of mass unemployment means spare capacity, the utilisation of which would result in growth. So, if the question is redefined in terms of *socially useful* growth and controls on the *rate* and *nature* of growth – with an acceptance that there are finite limits to the drain on natural resources and intolerable ecological side-effects of much modern technology – then a basis for common advance could be established.

Another fundamental foundation for a new approach is a commitment to feminism, which redefines every policy and is not relegated to a compartment somewhere down the policy list labelled 'women'. Socialist feminists in particular have redrawn the political agenda. Thus economic policy must encompass issues such as part-time work or flexible hours as well as child care facilities, instead of allowing these issues to be tackled as matters of social policy after the economy has been 'sorted out'.

Feminists have stressed a style of politics which is participatory and open, and they have demonstrated that the left will not be successful until we have addressed the concerns of the majority of people in Britain – women.

The Way Forward

The left is currently fragmented and lacking in confidence about how to defeat Thatcherism. Elements within it will exclude themselves from re-aligning the opposition: the sectarians and the posturers whose political attitudes are anachronistic and whose style is undemocratic.

It is also necessary to exclude an approach based on calling conferences to agree programmes. This approach is likely to founder on the rocks of nit-picking and semantics. The objectives should instead be to establish a common network for action and channels for dialogue.

This could become the basis of a popular crusade. Thatcherism is determined upon nothing less than the 'elimination of socialism' and the entrenchment of a free-wheeling capitalist culture which is turning Britain into an ugly, authoritarian and divided society. The stakes are very high.

Green Strategy

Sara Parkin

Strategy: noun: generalship, or the art of conducting a campaign and manoevering an army. From the Greek *stratos* meaning an army, and *agein*, to lead. Strategic position: a position that gives its holder a decisive advantage.

Chambers 20th Century Dictionary

I hope readers will bear with me if I stick with the unfortunate military aspect of the word strategy, since it provides a useful framework for the chapter. Like any general, I shall look at the objective and the timing of the campaign, conduct a review of the green troops, and then go on to look at the field of action itself, with its dangers and hostile territory as well as the high ground that Greens need to capture in order to gain a decisive advantage in their campaign.

It is also essential to set out quite clearly why we are going to battle in the first place. So many wars have been fought for nothing at all, so many lives have been sacrificed to revolutions that in the end changed very little, that it is as well to examine what is special about the green flag around which the troops are being asked to rally.

The Green Revolution

When *Silent Spring*, *Only One Earth* and *Blueprint for Survival* told me in 1972 that we are living beyond the means of the Earth and that the dilemma of humankind was one of survival, I believed them. I was deeply moved and became a fully paid up member of the green movement. Yet today I read in my newspaper: 'For the first time in the world's existence, a species – man – is causing a global change on a scale previously only seen with the onset of an ice age.' Although warnings about the 'greenhouse effect' to which the article was referring have been made for many years, all we have heard so far is a call for more detailed studies of the problem. The last fifteen years have done little to dispel my fear that we are more concerned with monitoring our own extinction than we are with avoiding it.

I am also conscious that most ordinary people do want to live in secure, convivial, non-polluted communities, and that they don't want to be menaced by dangerous technologies or weapons of mass destruction. The only argument seems to be about how to obtain such a lifestyle. We have managed to turn the world into a place where a huge majority of people are more or less dependent on a small minority; we have polluted the atmosphere so much that we are faced with grave climatic disturbances; and renewable resources like air, water, trees and soil are fast being turned into non-renewable resources. Although we imagined that increased travel and the concept of the global village would smooth away conflicts through knowledge and mutual understanding, the divisions between men and women, black and white, religions and cultures seem to have multiplied and deepened.

I have never been able to subscribe to the belief that our present predicament is the result of a plot sustained over several centuries, although I readily agree that it is the logical consequence of the consumer-driven industrial regime to which all of the rich and most of the not-so-rich countries of the world subscribe. My own diagnosis is that this regime has been constructed out of a series of wrong decisions – large and small, individual and collective – made over a considerable period of time. Building bombs instead of convivial life-sustaining communities, and failing to make our spirituality and our personal potential the real challenges of our life on Earth, are examples of how the human species has tended to gravitate towards the easier option at moments of choice and decision, whether they be practical or intellectual. In particular, by adopting the techniques of the scientific philosophers to develop our systems of economic and social organisation we have simplified the immeasurable muddle of human relationships, customs and beliefs to crisp, countable (and therefore totally unreal) columns in the accounts of social analysis. The environment in which all human activity *must* take place has been merely the white page on which these calculations are done. In short, we are living the consequences of a compound error.

Admitting to mistakes amongst our intimates is difficult enough. Admitting to a collective error committed over centuries will be even more difficult. It seems only sensible to seek the help of a strong guide and counsellor to help us restore our relationship with ourselves, each other and the planet to one of mutual respect and equal give and take. The only such counsellor that cannot be accused of manipulative self-interest is of course the Earth. Greens are suggesting that by abandoning our obsession with ourselves, and putting the Earth into the centre of all the models and plans we make for our personal and collective activities, we discover that, in the words of Theodore Roszak: 'The needs of the planet are the needs of the person . . . the rights of the person are the rights of the planet.'

Once conservation and protection of the Earth become the motor of our economic and social regime rather than the fuel for the present destructive, polluting consumer-driven industrial regime, it affects the health and well-being of not only the biosphere but of people too. Social justice becomes possible through conservation as it was never possible through consumption. For example, it becomes possible to measure satisfaction with our lives, our well-being – our 'success' – with real-life indicators such as health, cultural variety, clean air, safe water, healthy food, secure and convivial neighbourhoods and the number of species living there with us, rather than by what we consume expressed in very non-real indicators such as Gross National Product. Moreover, the currently fashionable but usually misused notions of 'green

growth' and 'sustainable development' take on their proper
meaning and logic when considered within the context of an
economic system based on the protection of the environment.
As there is a natural limit to what we may consume, but no
natural limit to what we may conserve and protect, models
for human activity based on nature remain valid for eternity.

The potential for using the environment as a key
negotiator in most, if not all, areas of human conflict is also
being developed. As a delegate at a recent meeting between
environmental groups in Central America put it: 'the search
for ecologically sustainable development is the same as working for peace.' He knows, through first hand experience, that
violence and oppression have never sustainably changed anything. The green revolution is, by definition, a nonviolent
one.

The flag around which Greens are asking people to rally
has EARTH FIRST writ large upon it, and the revolution we
are engaged upon is the replacement of the consumer-driven
industrial regime with a conserver-driven green one. The
campaign is to take this revolutionary message into every
corner of our personal lives and all our activities as quickly as
possible, in the clear understanding that our lives depend
upon it. The battle-cry of the Greens must not be for a new
ideology with which to govern our lives and each other, but
for a new attitude, a new approach to life which means we
may celebrate the diversity and the inspiration of the natural
world with ourselves as a part of it rather than apart from it.
Although the slogan for our campaign emphasises the centrality of the planet to green thinking, Greens are using nature
as a living reference book, not as a bible.

Objectives

The objective of the campaign then, is to green the planet.
And it is good to be quite clear that nothing less will do. It is
not sufficient to green *chez nous,* nor even the whole of
Europe, because it will not be sustainable unless the rest of
the world is greening around us. Although it is good to start

in our own back yard by 'acting locally and thinking globally', this favourite slogan of Greens should not become an
excuse to be parochial or isolationist. We have also to think
locally about how we may act globally.

We should also note the way in which the consumer-driven
industrial regime we seek to depose clings to its strategies,
despite mounting evidence of social disruption or imminent
ecological catastrophe. In the words of Mark Twain: 'When
they lost sight of their goals, they redoubled their efforts.'
Whatever strategies Greens do espouse, they must be sub-
jected to regular review to keep them on target and relevant
to the real and rapidly changing world.

Timescales

Greens love to talk about the future, but it is generally loose
and imprecise talk. Just how long have we got to green the
planet? My crystal ball is as muddy as most people's, but I
am prepared to make a rough guess. I reckon it will take
about a hundred years, but only if a serious start is made to
halting environmental destruction and degradation *within
the next decade.* To delay the start is to shorten the overall
timescale. For example, it is estimated that we destroy or
degrade about 20–24 million hectares of forest per year.
Delay in turning round this rate of tree loss not only affects
local economies and micro-climates, but is part of the pattern
that threatens the stability of the global atmosphere. We will
only find out how many trees are too few when it is already
too late.

What is certain is that we do not have an infinite amount
of time in which to examine the green fluff in our navels and
indulge ourselves in political pussyfooting or posturing. Talking timescales concentrates the mind wonderfully on the real
challenges the Greens face, and keeps more trivial preoccupa-
tions in perspective. All Greens should do it regularly, twice
daily before meals.

Review of the Troops

I like to think of the green movement as having four main divisions:

1. people who provide practical examples of how a green life-style might work, including organic farmers, people developing alternative technologies and so on;

2. single-issue pressure groups;

3. people who work by example or propaganda in the existing establishment – traditional political parties, churches, trades unions, universities and so on – or in their everyday lives; as sitting members of parliament, kings-in-waiting or mothers at the school gate, their contributions to the campaign will be varied but vital;

4. the distinctly green political parties.

Some Greens feel that we should concentrate on creating one homogeneous movement as soon as possible. I view this strategy as misguided and potentially catastrophic. Not only is the time not ripe, but we would lose the enormous strategic potential that lies in manoeuvering the four specialist divisions. Greens would be better occupied exploiting the extensive cross-membership that exists between the divisions of the green movement in order to develop sophisticated relationships – complementing instead of competing with each other, The pressure for change is greater if it comes from several different directions and, importantly, each division appeals to a different sort of recruit.

For example, it is not the job of the distinctly green parties to become the mirror image of the society they seek, nor should they try to emulate the single-issue pressure groups. The job of a green party is to develop and offer to the electorate a coherent and workable political programme that encompasses the demands of the pressure groups, and shows how the practical examples of the lifestyles movement can be brought into the political mainstream. This programme can then be used as a weapon, not only by pressure-groups to show that their demands are not inconsistent with the well-being of the whole community, but also by the courageous souls working for change inside traditional institutions and political parties – which gives them a vested interest in co-operating in order to make that programme as good and as coherent as possible.

On the continent of Europe, where Greens have been elected to several national parliaments, the different divisions of the movement have in some cases established very fruitful ways of working together. Researchers in universities have been pleased to undertake particular areas of research for the green parties: in economics, agriculture or peace-related issues for example. Parliamentarians of all hues have been taking more interest in the demands of pressure groups, and personalities from all walks of life rally around the green flag from time to time. Admittedly the triggering event has often been the entry of a green party into parliament, but it seems to me that the jungle warfare imposed by the British electoral system demands even better co-operation between the various divisions in this country.

Although the British Green Party is not able to make the same impact in terms of parliamentary seats that the German or Belgian Green Parties have been able to do, its association with the increasing success of green parties in other countries and its own regularly improving performance at local elections do mean that it has to be treated by all parties as a political threat of some significance. The broader green movement in Britain, and even the Green Party itself, have been unwise to neglect the possibilities of deploying the Green Party in broader strategies for promoting green ideas. A steady build-up of awareness of and respect for green ideas has to happen in all areas of British life to prepare for the moment when the closet greens can declare themselves, and the different divisions of the green movement can come together in a pincer movement for the final stages of the campaign. When that moment will be, and under what circumstnces it will occur, are unfortunately still a matter for speculation, but to be unprepared for it would be unforgivable.

The Field of Action

It is, of course, human beings we have to green – we are the ones out of step with the natural and the normal. The rest of the biosphere is already wise to the concept of ecological balance and, quite frankly, would probably get on a lot better without us. Green environmentalism is about adjusting our behaviour to fit in with our natural environment, not the other way round. The field of action for our campaign is therefore people and their societies.

The changes which Greens seek require a radical transformation not only of the way people organise themselves, but also of many of their long-established systems of values and beliefs. In party political terms this means we are trying to shift the political cleavage so it becomes a green/non-green one instead of a left/right one. This is not something that will be achieved from a chronic minority position. So, given our timescales, how do Greens gain support for their campaign from a majority of people as quickly as possible? There is no point in developing multilateralist's paralysis and refusing to start until everyone is ready to join us. Nor is it desirable to fall into the same trap as the other political formations have done, ending up with a constituency that has built-in obsolescence – any socialist party will explain the problems that can bring.

There is in fact one sustainable majority waiting for Greens, a section of society whose interests and whose values already receive top billing in green thinking – women. And how logical to go on and increase that majority by adding to it the section of society in which women have a massive vested interest and over which they have considerable influence – their children. The surveys that have been done on the green parties reveal that women and young people already make up an important part of their activists and electorates.

Apart from the mathematical sense of taking women as a starting point for the green campaign, there are other strategic reasons why the green movement should focus on women. Per

Gahrton, in a paper prepared for the 1987 European Green Congress, notes that 'there can be no doubt that men, middle-aged career men, are tremendously over-represented amongst those who have brought mankind to the brink of nuclear war and ecological disaster.' More directly, some women writers wonder if the exploitation and manipulation of nature and women by men could be, as Australian Ariel Sallah has suggested, 'one vast compensatory rage' for their 'rather small role in human reproduction.' Whether men are motivated by revenge or a confused notion that they must appear strong in order to be considered worthy of protecting their mothers, it seems likely that only women have the power to absolve them and make it clear that we don't need their sort of defence. Per Gahrton 'seriously doubts whether man will ever recover without a period of matriarchy.'

Women certainly need to be able to use the green movement to regain confidence in their considerable power to liberate, not simply women from men, but men from themselves and to re-establish the confidence of all of us in the wisdom of natural instincts and patterns of life. Marita Haibach, who was Die Grunen's Secretary of State for Women's Affairs in the Hessen State Parliament in Germany for two years up to 1987, established an experimental cross-party Women's Affairs Committee shortly after she was first elected to the State Parliament in 1982. After a year, women from all four parties in the parliament agreed that the committee should contnue. This example from Hessen is echoed by the experience of many green women elected into various levels of local government. Heidi Hautala of the Finnish Greens believes that this represents a kind of 'post-feminist' consciousness. Increasingly women are preferring to work together, even in mixed-sex environments, less because they want to create an identity against men and the male-oriented situations, but more because they want to create positive alternatives.

The Route

We have an objective, we know roughly how long the campaign might take, and we have identified the transformation of society as our field of action. Now we need a route. Although this is difficult to map out clearly, we can be certain it will pass through some pretty hostile territory, populated by many enemies who have an interest in maintaining their particular status quo. They will be ready to wipe out unwary or inexperienced green troops, and will not be averse to fighting dirty. Being nice and green does not turn you into a super-hero – it does not vaccinate you against the dirty tricks of others. But in this hostile territory there are some key strategic positions, high ground that, if captured, will give Greens decisive advantages.

Hostile Territory

The rise of support for right-wing authoritarian politics and the declining influence of libertarian and communitarian ideals is given as evidence of a general disintegration of political and cultural norms throughout Europe. Certainly the message from election after election in Europe has been a rightward drift of conservative and social democratic parties, and a rapid fall-off in support for the more left-wing parties. Not surprisingly there has been several calls for a renewal of the pure socialist message, and for another go at a 'red' revolution. Yet socialism, in all its shapes and forms, has failed to face up to what George Lichtheim calls the 'inherent conflict between two quite different and possibly irreconcilable goals: economic growth and social equality.' Although socialism has tried to topple the consumer-driven industrial regime by rationing its supply of compliant people, it has repeatedly failed to recognise the *pivotal* role of the environment in any successful revolution, and has never understood how important it is for any vision of the future to contain food for the spirit as well as the body.

Hard at work too, seeking to smother the Greens and convince the ordinary citizen that environmental protection is in good hands, are the sort of industries and institutions that grow fat in the climate of unrestrained consumption. ICI and

Shell International compete for awards for 'environmental excellence', and underwrite books such as John Elkington's *The Green Capitalists*, which 'reveals that the world's environmentalists no longer have a monopoly on environmental thinking,' and explores 'the ways in which leading companies in the oil industry, the chemical industry, the engineering industry and the biotechnology industry, to take just a few examples, have adapted to environmental constraints and are beginning, in many cases, to exploit environmental opportunities.' The environment industry has been born. Unfortunately it is not about consuming less, but about consuming differently. Underneath, business goes on as usual.

Surviving the combined attacks of socialism wanting to have just one more go, and the consumer-driven industrial regime deploying 'proactive strategies' in order to capture the 'frontiers of environmental science' for themselves, means that Greens will have to mount a vigorous defence of their ideas. Unsurprisingly, the best means of defence turns out to be attack.

This means that Greens will have to stop being squeamish about power. Ignoring it does not make it go away, it just falls into the wrong hands. Greens are actually deeply concerned about power. They are after all proposing the most radical redistribution of power and wealth ever contemplated, not merely between classes but between continents and between generations. These fine words can never become reality without manipulating power. Greens need to know where power is, who holds it and how it is being used, who is benefiting, who and what is being exploited. Only by becoming experts in the nature and dynamics of power will Greens be able to applaud when it is being used in ways that they approve of, and to shout 'foul' when it is abused. Only by becoming experts in the nature and dynamics of power can Greens hope to re-distribute it in ways that do not surprise us with undesirable side-effects.

Politicians are, of course, part of the power complex. But for green strategy it is helpful, particularly in Britain where the electoral system and the secrecy of government deny the majority of people access or influence over the important decisions that shape our society, to treat them like a protective cushion between the really big power-brokers and ordinary people – a cushion that needs to be punctured in order to expose the activities of the power-brokers to the critical gaze of the ordinary citizen. The vain search for a coherent set of policies relevant to today's pressing problems has forced the main political formations, in Britain as in other countries, away from their traditional positions and into the extreme corners of their ideologies. Increasing their discomfort, their *disarray*, exposing their ideological bankruptcy, is necessary if Greens wish to puncture the present political cushion beyond repair.

However, Greens must avoid falling into the revolutionaries' trap of assuming that they must wait until the consumer-driven industrial regime is a heap of ashes before setting up our conserver-driven green regime. By then it will already be too late. Rather than try to hasten the wholesale disintegration of the present regime, Greens would be wiser to carefully analyse its disarray. By all means let us seek to sabotage every wrong move made by our political leaders and our institutions, but we should put our *major effort* into pointing out, floodlighting even, any steps made in the right direction, whoever is proposing them. Green strategy must be re-constructionalist; we have no time to indulge ourselves overmuch with deconstructionalism.

Sadly the UK electoral system blunts the pin of smaller political parties like the Greens, but this makes it all the more important for the whole green movement to prioritise its battles according to their winnabilty, and to review the way it formulates its demands. Greens in all divisions need to ration their fondness for telling governments what they should do (which is a waste of time in the UK as they usually don't), and resist the growing tendency to write books and hold meetings aimed mostly at the already converted. Instead Greens should consistently look outwards, talk in terms that ordinary people can understand, and launch precise campaigns at the institutions and organisations that support the government's position.

For example, the post-Chernobyl anti-nuclear climate in most countries, the proposed privatisation of the British electricty industry, the further evidence of cancer around nuclear reprocessing plants, the age of the Magnox reactors in Britain, doubts about the fast-breeder programme and indications that the government is thinking about the alternative energy systems market, all suggest that the nuclear skirmish is one that could be won quite soon. The damage that such a win would do to the protective political cushion, and the boost it would give to the green troops, would be considerable. However the government *needs* the green movement to mobilise all its divisions to give it a pincer movement of excuses to capitulate.

Bickering over bequerels should give way to targetting women and their concern about their children. If the lambs in Cumbria are sill radioactive, what about all the contaminated milk and green foodstuff that went into the pig-troughs of Europe? Is the Euro-sausage a danger to my family's health? The Radiological Protection Board is supposed to have a strong consumer protection remit; is it monitoring my sausages? Stoking everyday doubts must always be accompanied by the *practical details* of the reasonable, possible alternative. Competent plans for shutting down nuclear power stations in the near future need to be elaborated openly and honestly, recruiting expert help and local knowledge and the support of opinion formers from all walks of life. Such plans also have to be related to the broader concepts of a low energy society and a conserver-driven green economy. Lobbying campaigns have to be mounted – of MPs in their constituencies, of experts in their academic circles, of farmers in their fields, of shoppers in the supermarket. And so on.

I can almost hear the grinding of teeth from anti-nuclear activists as I write this. But we're trying, we're trying, I hear you say, I know; I am trying too, but if nuclear power station-toting governments were thrown into disarray by the accident at Chernobyl, then the anti-nuclear movement in Europe was equally caught on the hop. When the golden opportunity came to put a floodlight on the positive details of a post-nuclear world, all we could come up with was a rag-bag of statements which boiled down to little more than 'yes, isn't it dreadful, but we did warn you.'

My point is that there is no way in which one division of the green movement can carry out the whole range of offensive actions that will be required to survive in hostile enemy territory, never mind win the anti-nuclear or any other significant skirmish. The green movement will succeed *only* if the specialist divisions share out the jobs according to the abilities of their foot-soldiers and the sort of territory over which they operate best. There is no need for rigid or formal battle plans. As the enemy has so well demonstrated, the most successful sort of co-ordination in these cases takes place in bars and restaurants. Let the old boy network be replaced by the new green one!

Strategic Positions

Knowing our enemies is one thing, but it is just as important for our campaign to understand how our potential friends tick. However much people may like the ideas of the Greens, and may even believe that our vision of the future is the only realistic one, they are understandably profoundly influenced by today's world, where consuming is cheaper than conserving and competing brings more rewards than co-operating. Opinion polls may show that the majority of people are worried about nuclear power and do want to live in a peaceful, ecological sound world. Yet they go on voting for pro-nuclear, military-minded, environmentally-blind governments. Greens would appear to have a long way to go to capture the ultimate strategic high ground where people perceive their best interests lie.

Paradoxically, I feel Greens could take some tips from the generally reviled advertisng industry. They would tell us that, in an age of Access and Barclaycard, our message of 'pay now, live later' is distinctly lacking in street-cred. Asking people who are addicted to a Nanny-state to 'Vote Green and Do-it-yourself' can be equally unappealing. We need to prepare a careful detoxification programme, and to consider more attractive ways of selling (selling, note, not compromising!) our policies. There is no need to stop preaching revolution, but let's make it very clear that the revolution is in people's hearts and minds, and that after that it is common sense all the way.

Greens are generally too reticent about discussing the philosophical revolution that underpins their thinking. 'The universe is no longer seen as a machine, made up of a multitude of separate objects, but appears as a harmonious indivisible whole; a network of dynamic relationships that includes the observer and his or her consciousness in an essential way' is how theoretical physicist Fritjof Capra describes the conceptual shift in which physical scientists are engaged. This new view of how the world works is beginning to permeate other sciences as well as the humanities and social sciences. Greens should be in the van of this intellectual movement, not least because it offers the solid logical high ground from which they can encourage people to cut their umbilical cords with the social, political and economic systems that are the natural children of the once-thought-to-be-exact physical sciences. The Greens should promote the common sense, workable package of policies that flow logically from their holistic analysis of the human predicament.

To make this possible, Greens need to capture the high ground of being perceived as politically competent. Taking the pomposity out of politics is an essential part of any green strategy, but it is not enough merely to debunk the myth that only grey-suited, narrowly educated men can be real politicians. Men (and women) can do politics in jeans and in jumpers, but they still have to be competent and worthy of people's trust and respect.

Neither should Greens neglect the high ground of the amazing inspiration and hope contained in the green vision of the future. Whether we like it or not, we all possess a spiritual dimension, and the Greens' celebration of the diversity and interconnectedness of all of nature has strong echoes of ancient wisdoms and cultures where spirituality played an important part. Today the search for spiritual satisfaction is taking people to extremist religions or in search of the ephemeral holy grail of consumerism. But many more are living with a spiritual void and the destructive apathy and despair that hopelessness can bring. If Greens wish to rekindle people's desire to take responsibility over their own lives, we have to relight the fires of spiritual hope too.

The Green Revolution

There is no doubt that the green revolution is under way. Since the first Green was elected to the Swiss parliament in 1979, he has been joined by colleagues in national parliaments in eight other countries – Belgium, Finland, Germany, Iceland, Australia, Luxembourg, Austria and Italy. In almost every country of west Europe there are Greens elected to some level of local government, and in countries where access to democracy is either proscribed or severely restricted, growing numbers of brave people are putting green ideas into practice in their everyday lives. In eastern Europe, for example, popular protest against severe environmental degradation is forcing governments to reconsider their position on basic human rights, and in Africa and Asia the conservation of trees, the development of a sustainable local economy and the rights of women are being skilfully deployed in concert in the cause of human survival. Awareness of the importance of a healthy life-sustaining environment has inspired the development of thousands of independent pressure groups and non-governmental organisations, and it pervades a growing number of institutions, even big-time environmental destroyers like the World Bank, dominating report after report on the future condition of human existence.

Such progress in such a short time is unprecedented in the history of revolutions. But does this mean that the green revolution is certan to be a successful one? Once again my crystal ball can give me no hint. It does, however, remind me that the green revolution has been triggered because the whole biosphere is in danger, and that if we get it wrong the first time, there will be no second chance. This is what Greens will have to keep at the front of their minds whatever strategies they adopt, wherever or whenever they are on active campaign. Otherwise they might become victims of the autolysis that afflicts all revolutionaries who do not care to see any further than their own barricades.

GREEN STRATEGY

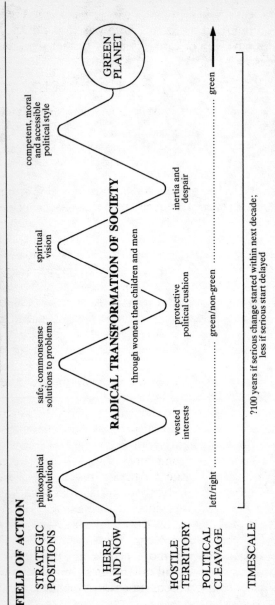

FIELD OF ACTION

STRATEGIC POSITIONS

HERE AND NOW — philosophical revolution — safe, commonsense solutions to problems — spiritual vision — competent, moral and accessible political style — GREEN PLANET

RADICAL TRANSFORMATION OF SOCIETY

through women then children and men

vested interests — protective political cushion — inertia and despair

HOSTILE TERRITORY

POLITICAL CLEAVAGE

left/right .... green

green/non-green .... green

TIMESCALE

?100 years if serious change started within next decade; less if serious start delayed

GREEN MOVEMENT

Lifestyles

Pressure Groups

Individual Propagandists

Green Parties

1   providing practical examples of how Green policies would work – organic farming, appropriate technologies, small schools, etc.
2   making specialist demands for healthy food, non-nuclear energy, human rights, peace, etc.
3   using programme of 4 and demands and examples of 1 and 2 to influence change wherever active
4   translating examples of 1 and demands of 2 into coherent, workable, political programmes with which to contest elections

The Politics of Realignment

Felix Dodds and Mike Harskin

It is difficult for Greens, Liberals and Socialists to look at politics in the 1980s without pessimism. Consistently losing elections can be depressing enough, but opponents of Thatcher's agenda have also lost nearly all the political arguments. The entrenched Conservative position in parliament is, if anything, an understatement of the 'grab it, own it, keep it' mentality that at times seems to have taken over the country. Thatcher has identified and encouraged a lifestyle that many people had already discovered for themselves. Her feat was in turning a trend into the overpowering political and social orthodoxy of our times. Fighting her, therefore, will need a new kind of politics.

There are, of course, many reasons to be optimistic. A few Socialists, Liberals (and Social Democrats) find cause for confidence in snail-like electoral advances. But the greatest changes have happened beyond the polling stations. Socialists would point to growing politicisation, a growing awareness of social and economic environments, brought on by great crusades like the miners' strike and the fight to save the GLC. Liberals and Greens might prefer to list Bob Geldof's fundraising with Band Aid and the global awareness he fostered amongst a new generation, or the tremendous growth of interest in environment and ecology. These events reflect the real change: that more and more people are prepared to become involved in what we still call 'politics', but which they see as individual or communal contributions to achieving what they cherish.

The greatest cause for optimism is the strength of these people, for none but the most extreme Thatcherite would claim to 'love' or 'cherish' the pursuit of money, while every campaigner for the environment, for development or for peace loves what they are doing, and cherishes the dream of success. Bobby Kennedy defined the difference in attitude when he said that 'Some see things as they are, and ask "Why?"; others dream of things that could be, and ask "Why not?"'

It is the growing number of people seeing the greed, exploitation and poverty, who then dream and campaign for compassion, mutual support and equality who are the politicians who will beat Thatcher.

The Growth of Community Politics

Liberals have long defined the process of individual and community politicisation as part of their approach to politics. This means working within and outside the established political institutions, such as parliament, and involves the concept of community, rather than class or economics based politics. The theory of community politics believes that it is not enough simply to lead, or to act as a representative for a community, but that the real breakthrough comes from educating and encouraging a community to tackle its own problems.

Peter Hain, when still in the Liberal Party, defined community politics as 'A style of political action through which people gain the confidence to mobilise for their rights and ability to control their lives. It involves cultivating in each individual the willingness to take direct action.' Community politicians believe that it is possible, and often more desirable, to achieve successes from outside the present system rather than becoming part of it as MPs or councillors. Direct pressure can be mounted on it from outside, or it can brought to bear by creating alternative structures.

In its simplest form, the Liberals would help to facilitate campaigns for a new pedestrian crossing by petitions, lobbying, demonstrations and other tactics, but in the last resort they would just paint zebra stripes across the road themselves. On a larger scale, the theory of community politics was employed in Liverpool, where the Liberals provided sufficient resources for council tenants to form co-operatives and design the sort of housing they wanted to live in, rather than enduring the concrete jungles that former Labour and Tory administrations had thought best for them.

A socialist equivalent was the organisation by miners' wives during the strike of 1984. They were often as critical of the way the strike was being run as they were of the National Coal Board. They established their own support structures, taking on political roles for the first time and achieving an enormous degree of personal development and liberation from the sexual stereotypes of tea- and home-makers. As one woman said, 'Being here, I see what women have to put up with. We're just unpaid bottle washers and cooks. I won't go back to just staying at home after the strike.'

Gaining control over one's own life is perhaps the key to community politics. It is the realisation that every individual has a potential to achieve change either working alone or, better still, working within a community. There are no necessary geographical barriers, and a community can exist at a workplace, or amongst an age group, or as a community of need, or as a nation or planet. The scale will depend upon the issue that needs to be faced. Overriding this is the acceptance that truly to experience freedom and individual liberty, an individual has a responsibility to ensure that others gain these freedoms as well.

This is mirrored by green attitudes towards direct democracy, and by many approaches to particular issues. The current thinking of most development agencies is that unless a community being 'helped' is learning to help itself – by using its own skills and resources – then outside aid can only be a compassionate form of imperialism. Similarly, a few planners and housing managers have come to realise that unless the inhabitants of housing estates are given the skills and then the power to take effective control of their housing management, simply putting window boxes on tower blocks or patching up areas of dry rot achieves nothing for tenants in the long term. It is this sort of thinking that should influence political progress as much as it has improved the quality of development programmes, housing regeneration and many other areas of life.

Community politics offers the strand of realignment that parallels the activities of pressure groups, where people can come together outside the present party political groupings to achieve change. It offers us the opportunity to rid ourselves of the political stereotypes that we carry with us due to our membership of particular political parties.

The Growth of Green Politics

Green politics has charted a similar rise in influence, and as with community politics it has come largely from the agitation of the 60s generation. More specifically, green politics developed from the increased awareness of all aspects of the environment. Many community politicians found that environmental improvement was the single greatest motivator for local people. Everything from planting trees and keeping streets clean, to fighting new road or office schemes and taking on the worst plans of the planners caused whole areas to become politicised, and many individuals to re-assess their own values.

At the same time, a coherent green message was emerging from writers such as Fritjof Capra and E.F. Schumacher, which echoed the gut feelings of many. Groups such as Greenpeace and Friends of the Earth were expanding rapidly, and early moves were made to establish a political platform for these new ideas. With the founding of the Ecology (now the Green) Party, unhappy green liberals or socialists found a more comfortable home which better articulated their own personal priorities.

The Green Party has struggled in an unfair electoral system, yet has attracted many thousands of activists, and has seen the election of Britain's first Green coucillors standing under that title. Levels of support, certainly in some areas such as the West Country, are no less respectable than those achieved by the most successful European green parties.

The influence on the established politicians has been substantial. Jonathon Porritt, as a former co-chair of the Green Party, adopted an open policy of pushing or pulling the other parties into line with a greener approach; in particular, as a former reluctant Liberal voter, he said 'It is my perception that of all the political parties in Britain, the Liberals are the most likely, both by temperament and by reason of political expedience, to move in a green direction.'

This certainly seemed to be the case until the formation of the Alliance. Liberals had led the parliamentary opposition to nuclear power under both Labour and Tory governments. They had come to accept, in 1979, the argument for a no-growth sustainable economy, in keeping with John Stuart Mill's arguments in 1848 for a stationary state of welfare and capital. The alliance with the SDP, however, turned them grey again, and took away Liberal opportunities for separate policy making. This left the Green Party with an even clearer field for its arguments, despite the many individual green liberals and socialists swimming against the tide in their own parties.

The Death of 'We Know Best'

Alongside the rise of community and green politics has been a steady growth in other social and political attitudes which are helpful to anti-Thatcherites. There is a growing healthy disrespect towards the old power structures upon which traditional, especially right-wing, politics depends. People are less likely to trust the media for a completely honest and even-handed view of events. They are less likely to put total faith in every policing or judicial policy. They are more cynical towards the 'we know best' merchants in the medical and legal professions or the 'we know everything' scientists and technocats who ran riot through the 1960s and 1970s. Most of all, more people are ready to fight back, and challenge what they feel to be wrong.

It is almost impossible nowadays for local and central government to get away with policies that went unnoticed for decades, without opposition from action groups. The overriding question is how to gather these feelings together in a political movement, however loosely defined, that can take on and defeat Thatcherism both at the ballot box and in the minds of the population of Britain.

The Electoral Arithmetic

In 1987, Labour Party supporters mounted what they felt was the best campaign of any party. It certainly won the pundits' votes, but its success was in retaining votes for the party, rather than in winning new supporters or even looking very deeply at the alternatives offered by a socialist agenda. The most typical response was an increased Labour majority in a seat that would have been safe anyway. The handful of seats that were gained were predominantly those lost in 1983 through incompetence, the 'surprise' factor of hard-working Tories, or re-drawn constituency boundaries (Oxford East is a good example).

For Liberals, the 1987 election was far less of a disaster than it seemed to most people at the time. Their vote had dipped, but the great majority of lost Alliance votes went in SDP-led seats. In many areas the Liberals made substantial progress and were left with more and better 'winnable' seats after the election than before. The 17 Liberal MPs matched exactly the 1983 total and, though still insignificant in parliamentary terms, was again the highest party total since 1935 (Labour's 229 MPs was the lowest, with the exception of 1983, since 1935).

Social Democrats had an appalling election, winning just five seats, one less than in 1983, and losing ground in all but a few of their targets. Even without the split between the Owenites and Mergerites, the SDP has a realistic chance of future victories in less than a dozen seats.

Greens entered the 1987 election campaign with few misconceptions about the state of democracy in this country. Unlike socialists and liberals, the Greens realise that they fight elections not necessarily to win, but to raise issues, set people thinking, and gain support for ideas rather than for manufactured candidates. This is altogether a better form of politics, but a much harder, longer, stonier path to follow – maybe too long a path in a world so full of nuclear weapons, social and economic deprivation, and ecological suicide bids.

There was little real evidence that either Labour, the Liberals or the Greens were capturing the next and youngest generations of the electorate. The German Greens now take 30% of the votes of those aged thirty or under. Even after their professionally packaged presentations to the 'youth' vote, the Labour Party fared worse than it had throughout much of the 1960s and 1970s. Liberals failed to motivate anything like the level of interest amongst younger voters that they should be aiming for.

The 1987 election left Thatcher in only a slightly less secure position than in 1983, and far more secure than when she took power in 1979. Just looking at London gives some idea of the mountain her opponents now have to climb. Across the capital the Tories would have to lose between fifteen and twenty seats to begin to be worried about their overall majority. It is a pipedream to expect the London electorate to follow our political hopes in the near future, without a major change in the way the combined opposition presents itself.

Even with all the discipline and self-sacrifice that Liberal and Labour party members have made to form coalitions, they have rarely won power. This century, the Conservatives have been in government for forty years on their own, and as senior partners in coalition for a further twenty years. Labour has only won five elections outright (1945, 1950, 1964, 1966 and October 1974), just two with a comfortable working majority, while the Liberals have won only once (1906). A pessimistic view of this century's political history, for radicals, is that the Tories have been the natural party of government, except where they have slipped up, been exhausted by too long a stretch of power, or been kept out of office by Labour-Liberal co-operation.

It may now be the time for politicians to declare their green credentials when standing for election to parliament and local authorities, so that the electorate can decide to elect green MPs whichever party they belong to.

The Problem with Parties

Disraeli said that Britain does not love coalitions, but this is only partially true. Coalitions have generally been turned to in times of war, or severe economic crises. Most lasting, though, have been the coalitions which have always existed within the political parties.

In order to survive and succeed as major political forces, both the post-war Labour and Conservative parties have tolerated a diversity of view that, in a better democracy (and in most of Europe) would have long ago split into many more competing and co-operating groups, each with their own identity, distinct manifesto and party structure.

Even with the breakdown of the consensus between Labour and Tory politicians on most issues throughout the 1950s, '60s and '70s, there is a marked overlap between the parties, and no less a diversity of view within them. Labour has members ranging from Trotskyists in Militant, through to conservatives in the electricians' union. The Tories have many wet liberals and social democrats, through to Powellites and extreme nationalists. The glue that holds these party-based coalitions together is the common rewards they gain with office, which is made more likely in Britain by being bigger and more united a political force than anyone else.

However, a significant proportion of the members of each of these parties, and to a lesser extent the Liberals, are being conned into staying loyal long after the actual or potential rewards of doing so compensate for the compromises they have to make. A few groups have realised this, and been on the verge of breaking away. The Bevanites in the Labour Party may have left if Labour had lost the 1964 election. More recently, Militant, which has never made an effective secret of its entryist nature, has been feeding off the Labour Party bulk until it is strong enough to break free. The Powellites in the Tory Party may have attempted to go it alone, as Mosley did. Many have found a new home in the NF and other far-right fringe parties.

Only the SDP in 1981 has split as a cohesive group, once they decided that the social democratic agenda was effectively dead and buried by the Wembley Special Conference of that year and the events that had led up to it. Ironically, the recent history of the Labour Party's policy review may leave many SDP supporters with a feeling of premature evacuation.

Significantly, the SDP straightaway sought co-operation with the Liberals, which they perceived to be a 'centre party' with broadly social democratic policies. Although radical successes such as the no-growth motion passed by Liberal Assembly in 1979 were beginning to change the party to be more in tune with its activist network of community politicians, the SDP's assessment was probably accurate. Some people characterised early Alliance problems by stating that the Liberals were being led by a social democrat, while the SDP were being led by a liberal (Roy Jenkins). In 1984, Cyril Smith MP went further and said: 'Steel is a social democrat . . . his aim is to destroy the Liberal Party in order to create a new centre party.'

The Alliance between Liberals and the SDP began to take on the shape of the broad coalitions existing within the Labour and Conservative parties. There was a general commonality of what was wrong, and widespread agreement on some short-term solutions. But on matters of philosophy, long term goals and the key motivation behind political activity, there were enormous, sometimes gaping, disagreements. The Alliance brought together the efficient managers of the SDP and the grassroots revolutionaries of the Liberal 'community politics' wing. The failure of the Alliance was its own inability to adapt to this kind of coalition politics – the kind of politics it said it wanted for the country, and that the country wanted.

Without doubt, any reasonable form of proportional representation would allow many of the separate streams in the three main parties to break away. British politics would follow a more European pattern, arguably a more normal pattern, with right-wing nationalist parties, some form of Christian Democrats, a centre/social democratic party, left-wing social democrats and democratic socialists in one party, a proper socialist party, communists, trotskyists, liberals and/or radicals, and greens. This division would be more honest in the choices it presented the public, and for the party homes it gave to the politicians. The arguments about stability and strong government are not proven on either side (West Germany is indisputably strong and stable due to coalition government, Italy is not). What cannot be in question is that a realignment of the political parties, through the introduction of PR or by a process of disintegration, would go a long way to achieving a better democracy.

This is a longer term view. Outside the Green Party Britain is unlikely to see properly socialist, properly liberal or properly anything else candidates at the next general election. The whole system of party coalitions and party politics in this country penalises those politicians who are most honest about their viewpoint, and rewards those who are most circumspect. The classic illustration was the pre-war Liberal MP in the East End, who always won by hinting to the Jewish voters that he was a Jew, while hinting to the Gentile voters he was a Gentile, without ever confirming or denying either perception.

What Next?

Political realignment of the sort described above will take time. It is not going to happen before the next general election, and another crushing defeat for Labour and the disappointment for the Liberals will see the strains of their party coalitions emerging stronger than before. If Thatcher loses and there is a balanced parliament, the price of SLD co-operation will certainly be PR. In any case, realignment towards a better democracy must not be based on the political ambition of a few party leaders, or on a reaction to events in Westminster (as the SDP, now with a chief and two Indians has shown). Instead, successful and lasting political realignment must arise from a grassroots desire for change, and action from below to build political movements that adequately reflect a point of view, philosophy or ideology. This is something that can start now.

In January 1988, Green Voice – a network of Greens and Liberals, not all of whom are members of the Green Party or SLD –

held its first gatherng to break down some of the barriers that exist between two political parties wishing to communicate, to investigate common ground and, just as importantly, grounds for disagreement. There has been a parallel dialogue between reds and greens. Both have built on the long-standing personal and political relationships that have already seen co-operation on a local level in many areas. Sarah Benton, writing in the January 1988 *New Statesman*, recognised the broader aims of the Green Voice gathering, reporting that 'This is a realignment not of the centre but of the left. It means regrouping all those environmentalists, anti-nuclear, freethinking spirits who dislike Labour's stodgy, hierarchical forms – the compromise Labour has made with the trade unions and state power – into a new alliance . . . It is a dream that has certanly seduced many socialists.'

The seduction of individual socialists is perhaps a harder task for a grassroots realignment than increasing the present levels of local co-operation between green Liberals and liberal Greens. We would argue, from a Liberal perspective, that there are few policy differences between radical Liberals and the Green Party, and the philosophical differences that exist are, generally, in relation to means rather than ends. Liberals and Greens both start from a social analysis that fits economic and other policies into their doctrine of sustainability, equality, liberty and participation. Socialists, however, start from an economic analysis, which tries to fit social and ecological progress into a fairly inflexible economic doctrine.

There are nevertheless many decentralist and green socialists who are prepared to work with others. Their numbers will increase substantially as more 'co-operators' come out of the closet, especially if Labour fails again to make electoral gains.

It is noticeable that both Green Voice and the Green Socialist Conference have been grassroot initiatives. Where they have involved well-known figures in the respective parties, it has been through their own choice, rather than the need for any sorts of 'leaders' for this process. Indeed, Simon Hughes, Liberal MP for Southwark and Bermondsey, made his own views clear at the first Green Voice gathering, when he said he would consider offering himself as a joint Green and Liberal candidate at the next election if the new Social and Liberal Democrats were not truly environmentalist, internationalist, devolutionary, communitarian and redistributive of unjustly shared resources. He felt that at least two other Liberal/SLD MPs would do likewise. Rather than seeking the Parliamentary road to realignment – patching up deals and coalitions – a new parliamentary grouping would thus evolve from the spread of ideas outside parliament.

The failing coalition within the Labour Party, and the possibility of a failure to hold together the different strands in the SLD, may lead to structural realignment towards new party labels and groupings (though not necessarily new parties), such as Green Socialist and Green Democrat. Much more significant will be the continued drift of disssatisfied members of all the parties, and those outside the existing party structures, towards greater co-operation. They may well unite around the sort of short-term agenda suggested by Peter Hain, or close variations of it. Central to such co-operation would be a demand for sustainable policies that draw the planet back from the most pressing eco- and environmental disasters it now faces; for a better democracy with some form of proportional representation and strengthened local and devolved forms of government; and for a social policy that makes good the worst effects of ten years under the Tories.

It is already clear that more people both inside and outside the political parties are prepared to co-operate on major single issue campaigns, such as fighting Poll Tax, winning greater power for the nations and regions of Britain, and campaigning for electoral reform. Much more co-operation exists at individual and local levels, in one-off campaigns in response to local environmental (and especially planning) issues. In a few places, there have even been tacit electoral deals between Liberals and Greens, as to which wards they should each fight in local elections.

The electoral arithmetic also points towards co-operation, as more and more local authorities become balanced or 'hung' with no party securing an overall majority. This, too, must be the most likely result of the 1991–2 General Election, rather than a fourth Tory win. A quarter of British local authorities are now balanced, with Liberal/SLD influence in more than a hundred of them. About twenty authorities, including many counties such as Bedfordshire, Cambridgeshire and Oxfordshire, rotate or share the committee chairs between parties, and a further sixty are operating without formal arrangements, but with such policy being passed or rejected on its merits. The increasing local experience of having to deal across party boundaries in order to achieve policies which are agreeable to more than one group has, generally, provided for good local government, and is far ahead of the crude party chauvinism in Westminster and the party HQs.

The major task for the next few years is to continue to lay the foundation for a principled and far-reaching realignment that may begin as soon as the next general election is over. Community politics offers many people the opportunity to join together and achieve changes in their community. Pressure groups hold the key to uniting people around common causes, and establishing national and international links. Even the political parties have a role, as their members begin to break down some of the most artificial party boundaries, recognising their own shortcomings and the contribution other strands of thought can make.

Green Voice's original publicity material asked Liberals if they envied the idealism of the Green Party, and Greens if they envied the ability to put at least some ideas into action as the Liberals have done. It is not so much a question of envy, but of sharing experience and enthusiasm, so that greens, liberals and socialists can work together more openly on the most urgent problems facing their communities.

The future is in our hands rather than those of the party leaders, and the crises of peace versus war, development versus despair, sustainability versus annihilation, are ours to solve. It is increasingly clear that the established parties are unable to meet these challenges, and a realignment of the kind we argue for cannot be postponed. As Martin Luther King said: 'We are faced with the fact that tomorrow is today. There is such a thing as being too late. Over the bleached bones of numerous civilisations are written the pathetic words "Too Late".'

Postscript:
Re-aligning the Vision

'If a man does not keep pace with his companions, perhaps it is because he hears a different drummer. Let him step to the music he hears, however measured or far away.' – *Henry Thoreau.*

Short of some vertiginous collapse of one or other of the Earth's life-support systems, the extent of genuinely green political realignment over the next decade will be strictly limited.

The power of those who now despoil the Earth and enslave, either conceptually or materially, the majority of humankind in the name of what they call 'progress', is still infinitely greater than the first flickering of green politics. Most people in the developed world really don't care very much about the environment, and the readiness even of those of goodwill to be bought off, co-opted or compromised remains disturbingly high.

There is no room for illusion about this state of affairs. Without realism, there is little point attempting to envision a different future, but with it, despite the mind-numbing anguish of the Earth and the numberless dispossessed, a new and hopeful vision is already beginning to emerge.

I believe such realistic hopefulness to be amply justified. All the contributors to this book see themselves in one way or another as 'Greens'. Ten years ago, such a designation would have been meaningless or vaguely disparaging. In just one decade, an international movement has taken root (albeit, until now, more in the North than the South, more in the West than the East), and through an extraordinary multiplicity of political parties, philosophers, artists, environmental organisations, writers, visionaries and practitioners of an ecological way of life, has begun to challenge the existing political order. In terms of diversity, early influence and the numbers of people already involved, let alone of future potential, there is little to contradict the claim that this multiplicity represents the single most important social and political movement since the birth of socialism.

The order that the Greens now challenge is the product of more than 200 years of global industrialism. During that time, systems of wealth creation and political organisation have gradually evolved which, from one perspective, have been astonishingly successful in progressively raising the material standard of living of many millions of people. From another, they have sown the seeds of self-destruction which we are even now beginning to harvest.

This is not the occasion to reiterate the catalogue of damage done and ruin threatening. The statistics are now more or less incontrovertible – to all but a tiny but disproportionately powerful minority of manic growthists and those with enough twisted honesty to acknowledge that their own personal gain depends on plundering the planet. The collective conclusion of literally thousands of authoritative reports is simple: our current way of life is unsustainable. We have already done grave damage by sustaining it thus far, and by seeking to sustain it, despite all the evidence, through into the next century, we wilfully and criminally put the prospects of future generations at terrible risk.

Given the capacity of certain commentators and politicians to abuse the English language, let me at once spell out that *unsustainable* means just that: sooner or later, we will not be able to go on living as we do now. Not a single contributor to this book will dissent from that statement; acceptance of it is the point at which each individual begins to see a little green.

The common ground between us, on that count alone, will therefore be extensive. And we would no doubt all agree that what matters most, at this stage, is the process of developing that broad consensus so that our first consideration is the distinction between green and non-green, rather than the distinction between different shades of green.

However, it has always been equally clear that even when a broad green consensus emerges, which it assuredly will, there will still be significantly different positions within it. To demonstrate simply what I mean, do you think it is the *totality* of our industrial way of life which is unsustainable, or certain *variations* of it (capitalist or communist, for example), or certain *features* of it, such as the indiscriminate pursuit of economic growth or inequitable patterns of international trade?

It is here that one finds the divergences between the different shades of green inevitably beginning to emerge. And that is still a wholly positive and constructive process, for without the investigation of such differences, the prospects for even some tokenistic realignment over the next decade are even slimmer.

From this point on, therefore, let me speak as an out-and-out Green. Not a socialist green, nor a liberal green, nor a green growthist. As such I don't much care to be told that the Democrats or the Labour Party, or some kind of reformed, mud-green version of industrialism are essential to the future of green politics. In reality, they remain highly prejudicial to that future. I say that partly on ideological grounds (though I do not happen to believe that the exquisite refining of a comprehensive green ideology is either necessary or desirable), but largely because the collective vision underpinning these different ideologies is itself unsustainable.

If realism is still the name of this uncomfortable game, then such points must be substantiated. The Democrats may eventually find a heart and a soul as well as a manifesto, but it will take years. Even as a non-Liberal, I truly regret the passing of the Liberal Party, for I understood why people joined that party and even why they gave their life to its service. There was real fire in their belly, even if the flames were fed a little too often by nostalgia. By contrast, the sole justification for joining the Democrats today would seem to be pragmatically, to split the difference between the Conservative Party and the Labour Party.

Though the visionary fire of the Liberal Party is now well and truly doused, one should never underestimate the capacity for renewal in any political organisation. Realistically, it's hard to see how that renewal can be anything other than green in essence.

As regards the Labour Party, the 1988 leadership debate did at least clarify the picture for green socialists. The original vision and impulse of socialism would seem to have been all but snuffed out in the UK. Failing the possibility of firing a new vision appropriate to the 21st century rather than the 20th, Mr Kinnock (quite understandably) has chosen to work within the confines of the old order, to mount an assault on the middle-ground by tweaking our consciences and promising capitalism with a human face.

Tony Benn is of course more aware of green politics than most of his colleagues in the Labour Party. But in the leadership election, he opted for the time-honoured time-warp of class warfare, nationalisation, the power of the trade unions, the politics of envy and what can only be described as a largely specious coalition of the dispossessed. Though Tony Benn talks green with genuine enthusiasm, integrity and commitment, his dogged adherence to such a platform *inevitably* marginalises any green element.

Between the two of them, green socialists have been well and truly nutcrackered. They will probably bounce back in the '90s, if for no other reason (and there may well be others – one should not be too cynical about the sincerity of green thinking in a significant minority of socialists) than Mr Kinnock and some of his more astute apparatchiks coming to realise that certain green issues will provide a useful channel for *safe* radicalism. The British public may have decided that a unilateralist party is unelectable, but support for nuclear power is now at its lowest ever. Consumers certainly do value the apparent 'choice' offered by our hypermarket economy, but they do not appreciate having their backyard so pungently dumped in in order to acquire that freedom of choice.

There is clearly a vast amount of confidence-building, consciousness-raising and baggage-shedding to be done along the way. From such a perspective, formal political realignment in the '90s is clearly going to be limited. The only factor which might affect this would be the introduction of proportional representation, though such speculative hopes would seem to have little to do with the kind of realism I am advocating.

At the same time, we must be especially alert to the political and moral ambivalence of some of today's trendier variations on the green theme. Green growth, green consumerism, green entrepreneurialism, green capitalism, green investment: you name it, someone's greened it. At one level, that's not such a bad thing, in that there's some merit in all of the above if advocated discriminatingly and practised sensitively. And little wonder, in Mrs Thatcher's Britain, that so many have creatively and convincingly adapted to the so-called 'spirit' of the times.

On balance, I believe that more good will be done than harm *if* one sees such an approach as part of a transitional strategy. After all, confronted with the choice between green yuppies or naturally nasty yuppies, between mindful green consumers or relatively mindless, old-style consumers, it's your proverbial Hobson's choice.

But let us not, even in the best interests of green solidarity, discount the ambivalence of such 'shallow ecology'. The problem about any transitional strategy is its potential to lull people into the belief that the getting there is the goal. Those who promulgate the benefits of green consumerism may themselves see it as but a step in the right direction; those who subsequently avail themselves of the benefits of green consumerism may be more inclined to see it as the end of the road. They may even suppose, consciously or subconsciously, that their consumptive conversion to the green cause will restore some kind of ecological balance.

It won't. Not in a millennium of green Sundays. At best, it may mitigate the most immediate symptoms of ecological decline, but the short-term advantages gained in the process are almost certainly outweighed by the simultaneous immunisation of such consumers against reality.

And there, of course, is the rub. Unsustainable means what it says. Green consumerism may marginally assist environmentalists in some of their campaigns, but its very effectiveness *depends* on not attempting to do down or supplant today's industrial order, and on not promoting awareness of its inherent unsustainability.

It also allows people to suppose that there is nothing wrong, philosophically or spiritually, with the way we relate to the Earth, just so long as we manage the Earth's resources more intelligently and efficiently. It allows people to suppose that their children and grandchildren may inherit a world in relatively good ecological nick, thanking us profusely for our enhanced sensitivity and foresight. It may even allow some people to suppose that such relative enlightenment will get the Third World off its murderous hook.

Those who support such drivel are even now enlisting as conscripts in the Green Movement's Trojan cavalry. Let us beware as they lay their alluring gifts at our weary feet.

If I sound a little exercised about this, it is only because I know the dilemma at first hand. One of Friends of the Earth's biggest successes over the last couple of years was its consumer campaign to persuade aerosol manufacturers to phase out the use of chlorofluorocarbons (CFCs) as propellants. (There is now no doubt that CFCs are primarily responsible for the thinning of the ozone layer which shields us from the sun's cancer-causing ultraviolet rays.) They really didn't want to know until we started distributing information about ozone-friendly aerosols, and threatening a major boycott of the eight largest companies involved. They then gave in completely, and even agreed to a labelling scheme which they had hitherto resisted with implacable hostility. By the end of 1989, between five and ten per cent of aerosols will be using CFCs; a few months ago, it was 70 per cent.

All good stuff – a small, incremental step towards a safer environment. But does it actually bring us anywhere nearer sustainability? Various deep Greens (including members of the Green Party) were quick to castigate Friends of the Earth for not campaigning against aerosols in general, inasmuch as they are indisputably unnecessary, wasteful and far from environmentally benign even if they don't use CFCs. Such critics suggested (and who can blame them?) that by campaigning *for* CFC-free aerosols, we were in fact condoning, if not positively promoting, self-indulgence, vanity and wholly unsustainable patterns of consumption.

As Director of Friends of the Earth, I know that we were right to campaign in the way we did. We would have made little, if any, headway with an anti-aerosol campaign. As an individual member of the Green Party, I felt distinctly worried about the long-term implications of what we were doing.

The reason why Friends of the Earth and all but a score of greener-than-green absolutists are put through the mill on such occasions is not so much a lack of vision in the Green Movement, as a lack of readiness to get out there and project that vision. If the future consists of nothing more than being able to tell the difference between an aerosol that uses CFCs and an aerosol that doesn't, then Gaia help us!

And that, I must be honest, is my profoundest hope – that the spirit of Gaia will spring up inspirationally in defence of those who now defend her. Even when taken metaphorically, such a statement will be seen by some as superstitious 'eco-lala' of the most disturbing kind. After all, if the spirit of the Earth moves at all, it assuredly does not move with any purpose, let alone with a capacity to hurl down green thunderbolts.

But such rationalists need take care, for reality is a harsh task-master. All the authors in this book would subscribe to a vision of an equitable, just and sustainable future. But there is in truth no realistic envisioning of an equitable, just and sustainable future which is premised on *any* variation of today's industrial, scientific materialism.

Any society in which an individual's power and self-determination resides almost exclusively in his/her capacity to consume, has renounced any serious effort to achieve justice between different nations, let alone between humankind and other species. Though equity does not entail absolutely equal shares, it certainly implies more or less fair shares for more or less everyone. That either means that our existing material standard of living will gradually become available to all five billion souls with whom we currently share this planet (let alone with the ten billion souls with whom we shall be sharing it by 2025), or it means that we should be prepared to reduce our own standard of living to the point where some approximation of equity may be achieved.

If you subscribe to the former view, then you cannot, by *definition*, subscribe to the principles of sustainability. Five billion people abusing the planet as we in the developed world do now – bearing in mind that it is *only* such uncompromising abuse which affords us such a high material standard of living – would precipitate irreparable ecological damage before we even get halfway through the next century. It you subscribe to the latter, you are deeply green, and thereby deeply outcast beyond any conventional political pale.

It remains extremely disturbing that so many all-but Greens refuse to face up to this central dilemma. Green Socialists and Democrats are only too keen to tell us, given continuing levels of poverty in Britain today, that it is impossible to talk about an end to industrial expansion and economic growth. The residual merit about Conservatism is that it is at least unapologetic about its manifestly inequitable, unsustainable and unjust politics. Would that such honesty were to be found elsewhere, for those who tell me that such a dilemma can be resolved through politics alone are being wilfully unrealistic.

Some may be depressed that a truly green vision cannot therefore be 'sold' politically. Others may take heart. Maybe it will encourage us to look a little deeper. The best spiritual leaders always seem to have known more about, and to be more committed to promoting, equity and social justice, and for that reason have often been the best politicians.

If metaphysics matters as much as physics, then it will probably become just as useful for those in the business of political realignment to be out there explaining why the old mechanistic world view of Bacon, Descartes and Newton is now wholly redundant (and correspondingly dangerous), as to be arguing the merits of flue gas desulphurisation. And if, in time, there develops a clearer consensus about the vision which Greens of every persuasion hold more or less in common than about the political means by which we might achieve that vision, then might we not, over the next decade, seek to build our movement around the vision rather than around the tactical process of achieving it?

This deepening out of the basis of green politics would already seem to have become indispensable. With the best will in the world, I can't help but conclude that many of today's green pragmatists, for all their assiduous efforts to manage the Earth's resources more wisely through the more efficient application of conventional reductionist science, so as to achieve 'sustainable' material progress for humankind, are in the unwitting process of selling Green politics down a very polluted river. A more holistic, Earth-centred vision of the world, in which spiritual values count for at least as much as the spur of materialism, has become a *precondition* for the emergence of genuinely sustainable systems of wealth creation. On a finite planet, the truth is that one cannot sustain that which one does not reverence.

Hence the need to step to the music we hear deep within us, and to argue in a forceful but conciliatory fashion that no political marching songs will be worth the raising of a single human voice if they do not harmonise with the song of the Earth.

Jonathon Porritt